2.25

THE GREAT REFORM BILL OF 1832

Liberal or Conservative?

PROBLEMS IN EUROPEAN CIVILIZATION

THE GREAT REFORM BILL OF 1832

Liberal or Conservative?

EDITED WITH AN INTRODUCTION BY

Gilbert A. Cahill

STATE UNIVERSITY OF NEW YORK
COLLEGE AT CORTLAND

D. C. HEATH AND COMPANY
A DIVISION OF
RAYTHEON EDUCATION COMPANY
LEXINGTON, MASSACHUSETTS

Table of Contents

v

Introduction

FROM A CONSTITUTIONAL point of view, the Reform Bill of 1832 was the most important single act in English history since 1688. The controversy over its passage was bitter and lengthy: Radicals saw the Bill as the measure which would usher in an age of political democracy; the Tories believed that it would lead to the subversion of the Irish Union, the Church of England, the House of Lords, and ultimately the Monarchy. The Whig, or liberal, and the Tory, or conservative, positions were clearly delineated during the debate on the Bill. The passage of time has brought some historical revision, but nevertheless the liberal and conservative traditions have continued to exert a singularly strong influence upon the imagination and interpretations of historians, as the title of a recent essay, "The Other Face of Reform," will attest.

Most American students have had their view of the Reform Bill of 1832 shaped by G. M. Trevelyan, whose conclusions are still widely current in the European history textbooks written by American authors. This distinctly liberal Whig interpretation of the Reform Bill has shown an amazing resiliency. The lasting appeal of Trevelyan's interpretation derives from his easy style, from his optimistic view of the historical process, from the confident sweep of his generalizations, and from the positive role he attributes to personality in the unwinding of history. He analyzes the weakness of the Duke of Wellington's position in Parliament as the result of the passage of Catholic emancipation, discusses the elements of the coalition which turned the Duke out on the issue of the Civil List, and emphasizes the growth of the middle class movement outside of Parliament and its ability to organize the currents of public opinion. Thereafter, he deals with Lord Grey's efforts to incline the King toward reform; to form a ministry favorable to reform; to appoint a Committee of Four to draft a sizable measure of reform; to commit the cabinet to the recommendations of the Committee of Four; to have Lord John Russell, rather than Henry Brougham, introduce the measure in the House of Commons. The result is a blend of personalized constitutional, political, and social history in which Lord Grey, an aristocratic leader, persuades the King and the aristocracy to accept a broad measure of parliamentary reform, to admit the middle classes to a share of political power by broadening the constitution, and to propose and finally pass the kind of bill that would have the support of public opinion, satisfy both the business and agricultural interests, and secure the acclaim of the nation. In Trevelyan's presentation, Lord Grey emerges as a patriot, loyal to his order, his country and his King, who correctly assessed the needs of his nation and who took the steps necessary to achieve his social and political goals. His vision avoided the danger of class revolution which threatened order on the continent, and extended the merits of the constitution to the aspiring middle classes.

G. Lowes Dickinson reenforces this interpretation of Trevelyan and has added that the Reform Act of 1832 was the first step in the transfer of power from a vigorous aristocracy to a democracy. The Reform Act was not forced upon the aristocracy by the people, but was deliberately introduced by the Whig section of the aristocracy and carried against the Tory section with the support of the people. The particular form the Reform Act took is attributable to two facts — that it was carried by the Whig aristocrats and that during the eighteenth and nineteenth centuries, a Whig opinion of the constitution had evolved. To the Whigs, there was nothing unsound about the structure of the constitution. They argued that while certain abuses existed, these abuses were rectifiable, specifically through a sizable reduction of the number of smaller boroughs. It was the members of these boroughs who sold themselves to the government and frustrated every attempt to legislate retrenchment and reform. Of this Whig view, the Act of 1832 is the clearest record. But the Whigs could not have carried the Bill without the support of the middle class. The agitation of 1832 was the movement of the middle class. The middle class were one with the King and the aristocracy in that they had no democratic ends, and wanted only to reform the constitution, not to transform it. The irony of history has revealed, however, that reform was just another term for transformation and but "the first step in an irresistible process towards democracy."

Over the years there has been no concerted attack upon the liberal Whig interpretation of the Reform Bill of 1832; this, however, is not to say that there have not been revisions. These modifications in interpretation have been made by both liberal and conservative historians: they have been partial and have been influenced by the particular historian's angle of history, his interest, and his period of concentration. For example, some historians have restudied the Reform Bill as the result of their concern with such areas of historical investigation as the structure of English politics, the role played by voluntary associations and public opinion in the politics of the 1830's and 1840's, or the problem of the continuing social and political power and prestige of the gentry and aristocracy throughout the nineteenth century. Other authors are concerned with the causes of

the Reform Bill, and still others with its consequences: but some look back at its consequences from 1914 or 1963, while still others view its effects from 1848; needless to say, the time factor often yields a different angle of vision.

Though the revisionists start from different angles and time periods in their approach to the Reform Bill, their areas of inquiry go back to certain explicit propositions of the liberal Whig interpretation. These areas of investigation deal with the following questions: (1) To what extent did the French Revolution act as a catalyst on the movement for parliamentary reform? (2) What part did social distress and the Catholic emancipation question play, by causing the turning out of the Wellington ministry, in bringing on the movement for parliamentary reform? (3) Did the agitators for parliamentary reform view it as an end in itself or as a means to an end and thus the harbinger of further reform? (4) Did the middle class start the agitation which led to the movement for parliamentary reform? (5) To what extent did the Reform of 1832 alter the class composition of the House of Commons? The first four questions deal with the causes of the Reform Bill of 1832. The last one, however, deals with the consequences of the Bill and can be tested by an analysis of the social composition of the post-Reform Bill Parliaments.

The year 1830 saw a revolution on the continent and was followed in England by a change of sovereign, an election, the turning out of the Wellington ministry, and the beginning of the movement for parliamentary reform. It is explicit in the liberal Whig interpretation that the French Revolution not only forced on the crisis in England, but was — as Wellington believed — a cause of the turning out of his ministry and the defeat of his party in the general election of 1830. In a thoughtful article, Norman Gash examines the relationship between "English Reform and French Revolution in the General Election of 1830." Professor Gash admits that the

French Revolution affected the propaganda of the Radicals, the ultra-Tories, and Henry Brougham, but finds as the result of a study of a number of contested elections that local issues were predominant in determining English political attitudes and behavior in the English elections of July and early August.

All writers on the Reform Bill are in agreement that the passage of Catholic emancipation brought about the split in the Tory party which led to the defection of the ultra-Tories and the turning out of the Wellington ministry. Recent scholarship has related the Catholic question to other issues, to the activities of interests, to the ideological basis of party, and even to the viability of the constitution. For example, Professor Asa Briggs in his *Age of Improvement* sees the Catholic question as one of a complex of issues and relates Catholic emancipation to two economic issues, Currency and the Corn Laws. From the termination of the Napoleonic wars, the three "C's" plagued the Liverpool ministry, as they continued to do the Canning and Wellington ministries, and during these years the landed interest came to identify its economic fate in a particular fashion with these three issues. The Corn Laws had been passed for the protection of the landed interest, but nevertheless agriculture continued in dire economic distress during the 1820's. This was so because in 1819, the Tory ministry had carried Robert Peel's Currency legislation. The protection offered by the Corn Laws was never able to counteract the deflation and economic depression experienced by the landed interest as the result of Currency reform. Thus within the Tory party, there came into being an ultra-Tory group, composed mostly of rural landowners, opposed to any relaxation of the Corn Laws, opposed to the ministry's deflationary Currency policy, and opposed to Catholic emancipation. To the ultra-Tories, any tampering with the Catholic question was the equivalent of treason and the subversion of the constitution, and possibly the opening wedge for repeal of the Corn Laws. This connection of the Catholic question with Currency and Corn in the ultra-Tory mind accounts for the explosive Tory reaction to the Wellington ministry upon the passage of Catholic emancipation.

Professor A. Aspinall's introduction to *Three Early Nineteenth Century Diaries* contains an interesting discussion of the background of the Reform Bill of 1832. He finds that the Wellington government had been a minority one ever since the passage of Catholic emancipation, and continued so after the election of 1830. Professor Aspinall continues with an analysis of the divisions within party, of the issues which promoted discontent, and of the nature of the opposition which turned out the Wellington ministry. He gives particular attention to the activities of the Marquess of Blandford, a spokesman for the Protestant and landed interest, and the ultra-Tories in initiating the movement for parliamentary reform; and to the way in which the ultra-Tories regarded the three issues of Currency reform, Corn and Catholic emancipation. In his view it was Parliament itself, and members of the Protestant and landed interests, who initiated the movement for parliamentary reform.

To the Whig aristocracy which carried the Reform Bill of 1832, the Bill was an end in itself. The measure was to be a final one, and Lord John Russell, who introduced the Bill in the House of Commons, was by 1839 known as "Finality Jack." The Whigs admitted the importance of public opinion, particularly of middle-class opinion, which by means of public meetings, petitions, and the press had secured considerable influence in the House of Commons. The Whigs, as Norman Gash has indicated, "were in effect asking the Tories not to surrender the powers of the aristocracy but to preserve those powers by opening their ranks and enlarging their basis." But to those who launched the agitation for reform, the Reform Bill was not an end in itself but a means to an end. The *Westminster Review*, which spoke for the advanced reformers, proclaimed this when it welcomed the change in the old composition of the House of Commons. The Reform Bill was defended not on principle, but as the best possible measure that the ministry could get passed. As the *Westminster Review* commented, "the discrepancies in the bill are less than the discrepancies existing in the system." The Bill was at best a compromise. The ministers were pledged to grant reform and had to effect it through legal means under the old constitutional system. This determined the kind of bill which the Whigs introduced in Parliament. A bill with too sweeping reform would have been resisted by the aristocracy, while if a sizable and comprehensive concesssion had not been made "the people would have risen in rebellion." The ministers had acted in accord with a universal manifestation of rational popular opinion, disseminated by the periodical press. According to the *Westminster Review,* this leveling of opinion augured well for the future of the nation. It promised the termination of the conflict between agricultural and industrial workers and the easement of the tensions between the two hostile classes and parties which promoted revolution in European nations. To the ministers, reform might be a final measure, but to the *Westminster Review* the Bill was but a step to the reform of other institutions.

The *Quarterly Review,* a Tory periodical, analyzed the revolution in the climate of opinion which had taken place as the result of the movement for parliamentary reform. The agitation was the work of a coalition of dissidents who saw reform as a means to the achievement of what the *Quarterly Review* considered incompatible goals. The *Quarterly Review* pointed out that from 1824 to 1829, not a single petition for parliamentary reform had been presented to Parliament, and yet within a period of several months the Movement Party had been able to rock the foundations of the constitution. The passage of Catholic emancipation, with its deleterious

effects upon the Tory party, was the starting point of the *Quarterly Review's* analysis. It noted that the public discussion of the Catholic question was first joined to the distress-of-the-nation issue by a small band of ultra-Tories. The successful revolution in France had created a fear of physical force among the middle and some of the upper classes in England. Against this background of revolution in France, the High Church Tories combined forces with the Birmingham Political Union and the demagogic efforts of Henry Brougham and Joseph Hume. These aggregate exertions kindled the revolutionary flame in England, and that flame, "thus fanned, spread, as was to be expected, in all directions." A pledge to support parliamentary reform was demanded of candidates at the hustings and as a result "an unusual proportion of Whigs and Radicals, many of them new to parliament, were returned." Rick burning and agricultural distress in Kent and a movement in Ireland for repeal of the Union broadened the scope of social unrest and "the cry for parliamentary reform, which had been sounded throughout the country, found an echo within the walls of the house itself." Newspapers and periodicals joined in intensifying the demand for reform and in stereotyped terms delineated the scapegoats of the campaign. The Whig ministry in early March made the agitation its own and thereafter petitions deluged the House of Commons.

In an article which appeared in the *Cambridge Historical Review* Professor Asa Briggs studied "The Background of the Parliamentary Reform Movement in Three English Cities (1830–2)." The cities investigated, all large unrepresented cities, are Birmingham, Manchester, and Leeds. "1830 saw the convergence of different local reform movements, each coloured by the social structure and political experience of its area." Professor Briggs sees the Whig Reform Bill not so much as an end in itself, but as a means to an end, the end varying with the interest groups existing within the community. In Birmingham, the Reform

Bill meant Currency reform; in Manchester, repeal of the Corn Laws; and in Leeds, factory reform. In this article, as in much of his other work, Professor Briggs has a keen awareness of the psychological factor; his analysis of the distress of the nation, the activities of reform organizations, and the significance and complexities of the currents of public opinion are major contributions. His reassessment of the involved nature of the historical dialectic of the reform movement bolsters and reaffirms the major propositions of the liberal Whig interpretation of the Reform Bill of 1832.

Clearly the two most explicit postulates of the liberal Whig interpretation of the Reform Bill are (1) that the middle classes were the prime movers in the agitation for parliamentary reform; and (2) that as a result of the Bill the landed interest and aristocracy shared its political power with the representatives of trade, commerce, and manufactures, thus altering the class composition of the House of Commons after 1832. It is with regard to these two propositions that the revisionists have been most successful in modifying the liberal Whig interpretation. Revisionists have noted that most of the provisions of the Whig Reform Bill were anticipated by the ultra-Tory *Blackwood's Edinburgh Magazine* in a series of three articles published between August 1829 and February 1831. These articles reveal that to the ultra-Tories the reform of the House of Commons was a means to an end, the preservation of the status quo, the continuance of the landed interests in power, and the maintenance of the Corn Laws; that the ultra-Tories were opposed to both the Wellington ministry and to the close borough interests; and that the ultra-Tories split with the Wellington-Peel ministry on the issue of Catholic emancipation, whose passage was attributed to Wellington's traffic with the close borough interests. In August 1829, *Blackwood's* gave testimony of this intra-party split by calling for a dissolution of Parliament. *Blackwood's* argued that the Wellington ministry had lost the confidence of

the nation by its gross apostasy on the Catholic question and by its indifference to public suffering and distress. The House of Commons, the argument continued, was largely devoid of patriotic men and composed of notoriously incompetent members. The change in the type of public servant, often legislating in direct opposition to public feeling, led *Blackwood's* to call for a reform of the House of Commons.

In February 1831, one month before the Whig ministry produced its plan of parliamentary reform, *Blackwood's* announced that all parties — Tories, Whigs, and Reformers — were favorable to reform. Many of the close boroughs were regularly sold, and since a single individual sold both seats of a borough to whomever he pleased, it was a matter of chance which party would benefit. *Blackwood's* continued that the system was defended because it worked well and to change it would lead to revolution. In actuality, the system worked in a pernicious manner: under it, Catholic emancipation had been passed, the petitions of the community had been ignored, and no action had been taken on the distress of the country. Moreover, over the years, in fact a silent revolution had taken place which put the "country gentlemen" and the landed interest at a serious disadvantage with other interests in the community. *Blackwood's* bewailed the fact that of late the landed interest had fallen upon lean days.

Aware that its political and ideological position had deteriorated as the result of the program of the Wellington-Peel ministry, the ultra-section of the Tory party started its political campaign to bolster the position of the landed interest. In this campaign of vituperation, the distress of the nation was attributed to political causes, to the policies of the Wellington-Peel ministry, and to the activities of the borough owners and the business interests — the very concert of interests which carried Catholic emancipation. *Blackwood's* pointed out that when Catholic emancipation was passed "it proved that a coalition of the great borough interests could make almost any change of law and institution in defiance of the public voice and the solemn engagements of the legislature." The close boroughs, the article continued, belonged to a few peers who used them for private gain. The peers sold them to the ministry and to the opposition. The boroughs were used against the country aristocracy, for "government has been acting for some time on the policy of basing itself more on trade and commerce and conciliating them (the business interests) by inroads upon agriculture — the great party aristocracy are ranging themselves more and more with trade and manufacturers — the latter are carrying on a war of extermination against agriculture and both the ministry and the opposition have embraced the doctrine that its continual though gradual sacrifice to them is necessary for the common good."

The result of this interpretation was to direct the popular antipathy occasioned by the passage of Catholic emancipation against the business interests and the borough owners. In this agitation, the ultra-Tories ascribed the distress of the agricultural interests to government by selfish interests which enriched the fundholders and placemen at the expense of the land. Reform of Parliament was advocated as the remedy for national suffering. As a consequence of this ultra-Tory interpretation of social unrest a distinction was drawn between the aristocratic political magnate or boroughmonger and the country aristocracy and the landed gentry. The aristocratic magnate who trafficked in close boroughs was differentiated from the landed aristocrat, who did not possess the luxury of the close borough and who often represented his county at a great financial cost. Such an interpretation also emphasized that the nation's misery was caused by a corrupt ministry maintained in power by the borough owners and the business interests. As the borough owner became the anti-symbol of the reform movement, groups and interests with incompatible goals were galvanized into action. The implications of

this line of argument are startling indeed, for it is central to *Blackwood's* position that the agitation for parliamentary reform was not initiated by the business interests and middle class, but by the landed interest, and that it was directed against the entrenched position of the business interests in the House of Commons.

The revisionists have been most successful in refuting the liberal Whig claim that as a consequence of the Bill the landed interest and aristocracy shared its political power with the business interests, thus altering the class composition of the House of Commons after 1832. In 1923, this aspect of the liberal Whig interpretation was questioned by Elie Halévy, who pointed out that the number of representatives of the business interests in the House of Commons "remained after 1832 practically the same as before." In 1938, S. F. Woolley quite convincingly upset the thesis that the Reform Bill admitted to the House of Commons an increased number of businessmen, who sat for the newly enfranchised cities and counties. He concluded that the business interests had greater representation prior to 1832 than they had in the Parliament of 1833, that in fact in the latter Parliament their number was substantially decreased. This diminution was traced to the demise of many close boroughs which to a very great extent had been the preserve of the business interests. Moreover, very few dissenters and non-conformists appeared in the new Parliament. The landed gentry and the landed aristocracy, in 1833 and after that date, continued to represent not only the counties in which they resided, but also many of the cities which received additional seats in 1832.

In 1954, Professor William O. Aydelotte published an interim report on his study of the Parliament of 1841–1847. In this statistical study of the 800 and more men who sat in the House of Commons during the life of this Parliament, Professor Aydelotte raises the following three questions: (1) How extensively had "middle class" or "business" elements penetrated into Parliament by the 1840's? (2) How far did these elements constitute a distinct group, clearly separate from the landed interest? (3) What social and economic groups were most prominent in each of the various parties? Professor Aydelotte's research reveals that the Parliament of 1841–1847 "was heavily dominated, in numbers at least, by the nobility, baronetage and landed gentry and their relatives." The number of "businessmen" proved to add up to a core of 123 men, a number about the same as that reported by S. F. Woolley in the pre-Reform Bill Parliament of 1830. Professor Aydelotte's findings are of interest, for they show that the Conservatives as a group were more closely related to the aristocracy and landed gentry than the Whigs and Reformers as a whole; that the two kinds of Conservatives, Peelites and other Conservatives, are surprisingly alike "in the amount of business interests"; and that the men with business interests in the Parliament of 1841–1847 were divided "almost equally between the conservative group and the general group composed of Whigs, Liberals and Reformers."

In a discerning article, "The Repeal of the Corn Laws and the Politics of the Forties," Professor G. Kitson Clark raises questions about the political behavior of the aristocracy and the landed gentry. He finds that the House of Commons in 1846 was essentially conservative and was dominated by the aristocracy, their sons, and the landed gentry; that contrary to what has been emphasized by historians, the Corn Laws were repealed not by the business interests, but by the aristocracy, entrenched in both the House of Commons and the House of Lords; and that by 1846 both the Whig opposition leaders as well as the conservative governmental leaders were favorable to repeal of the Corn Laws, and what political opposition there was came from the counties and the tenant-farmer electorate therein. Professor Kitson Clark's work is a testimonial to the vigor of the aristocracy and landed gentry. He denies that the repeal of the Corn Laws can be interpreted

"in any simple sense" as a chapter in the "victory of the middle class." Finally, by a series of masterful questions, he suggests that Corn Law repeal may be seen as a "'concession by the aristocracy', a timely retreat, that is, from a forward position which had proved to be dangerous," and that the removal of the emotive symbol of the bread tax may have slowed down the middle-class movements for extension of the suffrage, the reform of the House of Lords, and the disestablishment of the Church of England.

It is against this evolutionary history of revisionism that Professor D. C. Moore's "The Other Face of Reform" is to be assessed. For our purpose, this essay, as the title suggests, becomes an overall statement of the conservative position, and with it the argument has turned full circle on the liberal Whig thesis. The author maintains that it is a mistake, in the continental tradition, to equate reform and revolution. Parliamentary vote rather than revolution established political democracy in Britain, and each reform of Parliament was carried by an unreformed Parliament. Professor Moore concludes that the British experience "would therefore seem to require a separate interpretative framework." He rejects the view that the Reform Bill was a concession by which the ruling classes, by sharing power with the middle classes, avoided revolution. He also plays down the effect of the French Revolution upon the English elections of 1830. The demand for reform, he finds, emerged from hibernation, not in 1830, but in 1829 as the result of the opposition of many ultra-Tories and members of the country party to Wellington's passage of Catholic emancipation. It was not "the support of the masses" but the shift in the electoral behavior of the voters in the open and county constituencies which brought the Whigs to power in 1830 and 1831. Professor Moore's analysis of the poll books and issues in a number of county elections reveals that rural and urban opposition to the Wellington ministry were not opposed but allied. Ultra-

Tories who remembered the apostasy of Catholic emancipation and resisted any relaxation of the Corn Laws were in alliance with Thomas Attwood's middle-class Currency reformers. By 1830, deflation and distress had become the paramount issues. Professor Moore also notes a certain ambivalence in the Reform Bill of 1832. If it gave added political power to the middle classes in the newly created city constituencies, the Bill also restored the political power of the landed interests by ensuring control by these interests over the eighty-two old county seats as well as the sixty-four county seats created by the Bill. In a perceptive conclusion, Professor Moore adds that the Reform Bill agitation terminated the working agreement that existed between the Benthamites and the Wellington ministry and most likely "delayed such measures as the repeal of the Corn Laws."

The selections offered here are at best a sample of the vast literature on the Reform Bill of 1832. The sheer mass of materials and the countless questions raised by scholars of these materials might lead the student to dismiss the whole discussion as a pointless academicians' quarrel. Yet a close reading of the selections included in this volume reveals a surprisingly large area of agreement between adherents of the liberal and conservative schools of interpretation. Both liberals and conservatives underline the importance of the Corn, Currency, and Catholic issues; the discontent of various interest groups with the deflation and social distress of the 1820's; and the immediacy of the Catholic question in destroying the Wellington ministry's numerical majority in the House of Commons. There is also consensus that there was considerable party fragmentation both before and during the campaign for parliamentary reform; that both Whigs and ultra-Tories were concerned with a fairer representation of interests; that there was a strong middle-class and radical support for reform in the unrepresented cities; that it was the Protestant ultra-Tories and the "Country Party," the spokesmen for the landed interest, that

started the campaign that brought down the Wellington ministry. There is likewise general concurrence that conflicts of influential groups and interests within the social structure made it possible for dissident groups, both at the local and national levels, to make common cause against the Wellington ministry and to regard parliamentary reform as a means to diverse ends; that the French Revolution had relatively little effect upon the election of 1830; that the county constituencies, the stronghold of the landed interest, swung the parliamentary majority in favor of Lord Grey's ministry in the election of 1831; that public opinion was an influential factor, particularly in bringing pressure upon the House of Lords to accept reform. There is also a large degree of interpretative agreement concerning Lord Grey's tactics with the King, his Cabinet, his Committee of Four, and Henry Brougham, as well as his decision to carry a bold and comprehensive measure and the essentially aristocratic and conservative nature of the Bill.

Despite this wide range of agreement with regard to the significant areas of investigation in the movement for parliamentary reform, the interpretations of historians continue to display largely a liberal or a conservative emphasis. As previously noted, this may derive from the materials or the particular chronological period or event that the historian has investigated in depth, or from his view of the historical dialectic or the specific angle from which he approaches his materials. But 1832 is a point at which history did turn, and in Professor Collingwood's terminology, 1832 is a "nodal" date. Therefore, it may be well to ask some questions not raised by the authors of the articles and excerpts in this pamphlet. The student might well ask, Which borough owners were deprived of their close borough holdings? What proportion of them were Whig? What proportion were Tory? Did members of the business interest own close boroughs? What proportion of them lost their holdings? A number of questions could be raised about party organization and ideology both immediately before and after the passage of the Reform Bill. Why was party organization so weak before and after 1832? What prevented the formation of firm party lines after 1832? To what extent were party leaders and followers doctrinaire Liberals and Conservatives both before and after 1832? To what extent could the constituencies, boroughs, cities, and counties bring pressure to bear upon their representatives both before and after the Reform Bill of 1832? Another series of questions could be asked about the importance of public opinion in the movement for parliamentary reform. Did the ultra-Tories limit their political activities to the House of Commons or did they take their attack on Peel and Wellington to the rural and agricultural constituencies? What accounts for changes in a national climate of opinion? What part does liberalism and conservatism play in this change? How important were voluntary associations in structuring opinion, and what is the relationship between voluntary associations, the press and the government? If the press is a key area for study, what would constitute an adequate methodology for such a study? And certainly questions could be raised about the propriety of equating the middle classes with the business interests. Why were the numbers of the business interests much the same in 1846 as in the pre-Reform Bill Parliament? Why should it be assumed that the middle classes would elect members of the business interests? Were the dominant motives and loyalties of the middle classes economic, religious, or nationalist? What were the social aspirations of the business interests? Was there a single monolithic agricultural interest? The answers to these and other questions, it is hoped, will give the student a firmer grasp of the historical process and perhaps shed light upon the dialectic between liberalism and conservatism which is still very much with us at the present time.

The Conflict of Opinion

"When the King called the Bill 'an aristocratical measure,' the Tories laughed bitterly and accused Grey of playing upon his simplicity. Yet in persuading the King that the Bill would save the throne and the aristocracy and prevent bloodshed, Grey spoke his own honest belief, which turned out to be correct."

—— George Macaulay Trevelyan

"The real supporters of the Bill of 1832 were the middle class... By that measure the middle class were admitted to the franchise; they would exercise henceforth an important influence on the Lower House, and would have the redress of their grievances in their own hands."

—— G. Lowes Dickinson

"... one of the most disappointing features of the reformed parliament, from the point of view of the middle and lower middle classes, was the comparative fewness of the Radical members returned and the essential moderation of the parliament as a whole."

—— S. F. Woolley

"The British House of Commons had been reformed in 1832, but in truth the eighteenth century still stalked many of the constituencies of Great Britain and Ireland, if not quite naked, still as ever unashamed.... Moreover, the distribution of seats grossly favored the aristocracy and it grossly favored agriculture."

—— G. Kitson Clark

"All parties have long been the avowed friends of Reform; even the Tories, who profess the most decided opposition to it, have still their own plan, to which they give its name; on their declarations, they, as well as the Radicals, are Reformers. . . ."

—— Blackwood's Edinburgh Magazine

"Advantage was taken of these circumstances to revive the cry for parliamentary reform; and the note was first sounded . . . from a small band of the High Tories, whom the measures of the government had so deeply offended . . ."

—— Quarterly Review

"Wellington . . . attributed his defeat to two events; the July Revolution in France, and the concession of Catholic emancipation. . . . In many constituencies, therefore, he added, candidates were required to pledge themselves to vote for parliamentary reform and a policy of retrenchment."

—— A. A. Aspinall

"Neither before nor after the election did the government command a majority in the House of Commons. . . . Seen in detail, the most striking feature . . . is the importance of local and personal factors, and of domestic issues, rather than any signs of external stimulus."

—— Norman Gash

". . . it is impossible to set up any clear general distinction between the nobility and gentry on the one hand and those engaged in business on the other. . . . In the present state of knowledge it may be more to the point to reach a basis of fact which compels us to look critically to the intellectual framework in which we have been accustomed to discuss this period, to jettison catch-phrases, and to appreciate more deeply the difficulties of generalization."

—— William O. Aydelotte

". . . the first Reform Act did not mark a clear break in English political life. Least of all did it mark the arrival of the urban middle class to political power."

—— D. C. Moore

I. THE WHIG INTERPRETATION

The Whig Triumph

GEORGE MACAULAY TREVELYAN

George Macaulay Trevelyan (1876–1962), grand-nephew of the historian
Thomas Babington Macaulay and Regius Professor of Modern History at
Cambridge University until his death, has written widely in English social and
political history. Among his works on nineteenth-century England are *British
History in the Nineteenth Century and After, 1782–1919* (1937), *The Life of
John Bright* (1913), and *Lord Grey and the Reform Bill* (1920). This last book
is a classic in the literature of the reform bill struggle. In this selection from it,
Trevelyan deals with Lord Grey as a reform minister, whose vision avoided the
danger of class revolution and extended the merits of the constitution to the
aspiring middle class.

To THE MEN on whom fell the task of
enfranchising the working class in
the following generation, to the Chartists
and to John Bright after them, the most
important aspect of the First Reform Bill
was its limitations. But in the days of their
fathers, to Radical and Tory alike, the
miracle to be explained was why it went
so far. And that is the question that presents itself to History. The answer is given
by Mr. Butler, whose researches have provided for the first time a reliable and comprehensive history of the Bill and its passage:

Lord Grey's statesmanlike conviction of the
need and advantage of an extensive measure
was the prime source of the Bill; the wisdom
of Russell and the will of Durham embodied
this conviction in a bold and simple form; and
as regards the moderates in the Cabinet and
the party generally, it was proved once again
that a keen and determined minority will by
their very momentum overbear a comparatively indifferent and undecided majority.

It only needs to be added to this, that the
conversion of the "moderates in the party"
outside the Cabinet was effected by the
persuasive and terrifying expression of the
national will after the Bill had appeared
in public.

But until the measure had been drawn
up in secret, and accepted by a conservative King and a mixed Cabinet, its makers
had to work in the dark, uncheered by the
popular approval, and guided solely by
their own foresight of what the reception
of particular proposals was likely to be. It
was during these months of gestation before
the Bill saw light, from the end of November 1830 to the end of February 1831, that
Grey's tact and statecraft were put to their
severest test, and won a triumph so smooth
and perfect that the pitfalls and dangers he
avoided with such skill have scarcely been
noticed by posterity.

When, about a week after the comple-
tion of his Ministry, Grey asked Durham,
as they came down the steps of the House

From G. M. Trevelyan, *Lord Grey and the Reform Bill* (London, 1920), pp. 261–272, 274–279. Reprinted by permission of Longmans, Green & Company, Ltd.

1

of Lords, to "assist him in drawing up a Reform Bill" and to take Lord John Russell into partnership in the enterprise, he deliberately gave the key of the position to the advanced section of Reformers in his Cabinet. When, a few days later, he consented to the proposal of Durham and Russell that the "Committee of Four" to draw up the Bill should include besides themselves Sir James Graham and Lord Duncannon, the former closely confederate with Althorp, and the latter versed in the lore of Irish boroughs, deliberate exclusion had been made of all "moderates" and adherents of "bit by bit Reform."

No less marked was the exclusion of Brougham from these inner counsels. The Chancellor would have ruined all, for, while still regarded as the popular champion of Reform, he was wedded to the retention of half the rotten borough representation. And he would certainly have quarrelled on the Committee with Durham and Russell in particular, and in general with any colleague who tried to do business with him on equal terms. In the rivalry between Brougham and Russell for the leading place among Reformers, Grey had wisely sided with Russell. . . .

During December and January 1830–1, while the Bill was in the making, there was no shadow of ill-feeling between the men who were making it. The Committee of Four consulted deeply with Grey and Althorp. . . .

Since Russell was destined to introduce the Bill to the public in the House of Commons, Durham generously asked him to draw up the first "plan." Lord John's plan became the basis of the Committee's work, and remains the outline, with very little alteration in principle, of the Bill that passed into law. Lord John wrote that when he was drafting his plan, two considerations decided him in favour of a sweeping measure, "the authority of Lord Grey," and "the dangerous excitement consequent on the Duke of Wellington's denial of all Reform." The most important principles of the Bill—destruction of the rotten boroughs *en masse* without money compensation, and an uniform middle-class franchise for all boroughs old and new — though they were first set down on paper in the solitude of Lord John's study, were the result of informal conversations, extending over a period of many months, held between the Whig chiefs, especially Grey, Durham, Althorp, Ellice, and Lord John himself, the group whence emanated the Reform Bill. . . .

Anyone familiar with the political history of England from the Restoration of Charles II to the death of Queen Anne must be struck by the regular way in which successive general elections then gave effect to the variations of political opinion in the community. The alternation of Whig and Tory Parliaments in the reigns of the last Stuarts answered so happily and so accurately to the changing feelings of the public, that England was able to enforce her will in every big question as it came up — in Marlborough's time, for instance, the country was able to use the Whigs to win the war, the Tories to make the peace, and afterwards the Whigs again to secure the Hanoverian succession.

But during the seventy years before the Reform Bill things were very different. Throughout that period, increasingly as time went on, the country failed to make its wishes felt, whenever they conflicted with those of the King and of the borough-owners. Public opinion had not the means to continue Chatham in power; to stop the quarrel with America; to punish the Peterloo Ministry for passing the Six Acts and for prosecuting Queen Caroline. The Tories, however unpopular they might be, had no longer anything to fear, nor the Whigs anything to hope, from a general election. Only when at last a King not unfavourable to the Whigs chanced to ascend the throne, at a moment when the Tories were split up into three mutually hostile factions, could Grey and his friends obtain a precarious hold on power, conceded to them with almost contemptuous indifference, as to caretakers who must soon hand back the government of England to the men who owned it as their private property.

The Constitution then had changed in a non-popular direction. The Whigs were right in their historical argument that the "old constitution" which the Tories identified with the rotten boroughs was only about a century old in its methods and spirit, however mediaeval it might be in its form. It was the same, yet not the same. The reasons were clear. The population had gradually shifted from the old boroughs to new centres, and during the last forty years it had shifted with the increasing speed of great economic change. North England was insufficiently represented, and the new "industrial north" was hardly represented at all. That Old Sarum had two votes and Manchester none was important, not as a singularity, but as a symbol of the general state of the representation.

Indeed, although the names of the boroughs had been preserved without alteration since Stuart times, the position and character of the electorate had in many cases been changed, and changed for the worse. The process of bringing the borough elections under the control of small oligarchies in the borough, or of aristocratic influences outside, had been going on throughout the Tudor and Stuart periods; but it was only in the eighteenth century that the process had been completed, and that the position of a single borough "patron" had been publicly recognised in the majority of cases.

The variety of the franchise in the close boroughs was very great, but in effect each close borough belonged to one individual borough-owner, who was in a position to dictate or purchase the votes of the nominal electors. The borough-owner in his turn extracted from the Government of the day office, pensions, peerages, sinecures, and every form of advancement at the public expense for himself, his clients, and his relations. . . .

The men who drew up the Reform Bill determined to sweep away at one stroke all the "nomination boroughs" — that is, to substitute the principle of election by the people for that of nomination by a borough-owner in a good many more than 200 seats. This revolution was to be achieved by two distinct processes — first, by disfranchising all boroughs where the population was below a certain number, so taking away some 160 seats that could be used to enfranchise new boroughs and to add to the insufficient county representation; and secondly, by "opening" to all £10 householders the franchise of those "close boroughs" whose population justified their retaining one or more members.

The Reform Bill, in the eyes of the sufferers, was first and foremost a confiscation of private property and of corporate and customary rights, as extensive as that which accompanied the destruction of the mediaeval Church by the Tudors, and of the Monarchy by the victorious Roundheads. And this wholesale destruction of the property and influence of individuals was to be effected without compensation, though compensation had been part of the Reform schemes of Wyvill and Pitt half a century before, and of Russell himself in 1823. But in 1831 the country, already furious against the Whigs for their failure to retrench and for their refusal to abolish the life-pensions granted by the Tories, would have lost all patience if asked to buy out the "borough-mongers," the name by which the unfortunate borough-owners were execrated that year by nine Englishmen out of ten. . . .

Although the total abolition of nomination boroughs was at once the most popular and the most fiercely contested part of the Bill, it is the part that has been least questioned in the retrospect. The choice of the uniform £10 household franchise for all boroughs is open to more dispute; yet I believe that the more closely the actual conditions of that day are studied, the harder it becomes to name any alternative which would not have led to disaster.

First, it is suggested that the working class should have been enfranchised by an uniform household suffrage. The answer to this is that such a Bill would never have passed, and indeed owing to William IV's insurmountable objection to Radical Reform could never even have been introduced. The King, the two Houses of Parliament, and the middle classes would have been united against it. . . .

Secondly, it has been argued by more conservative temperaments like Peel, Disraeli, and Bagehot that there ought to have been no uniform suffrage at all, but a variety of different franchises. It was plausibly and honestly argued by Peel in 1831 that it was a grave evil to abolish the working-class electorate in Preston and Westminster in favour of the £10 householder; that the new franchise should have been made to vary from place to place, democratic here, middle-class there, aristocratic or "borough-mongering" elsewhere. This doctrine still finds advocates. England, it is argued, should have been represented by her different classes, instead of being swamped first by a middle class, and thirty-five years later by a lower class electorate. . . .

But even those who think that the uniform franchises of 1832, 1867, 1884, and 1917 have been a series of misfortunes, or at least of chances of perfection let slip owing to the original error of 1831, must answer the question which Grey and the Committee of Four had to ask themselves — how can the establishment of "fancy" and "variety" franchises be defended in the House and in the country? How, the Whig statesmen may well have thought, can we confiscate vast masses of property purchased or inherited, and then turn round and create at our own whim and fancy new privileges, picking here and choosing there which rotten boroughs are to survive, which towns shall have household suffrage, which shall have a £10, a £20 or an educational franchise? Unless we have one rule to apply to all cases, the charge of "cooking" in the Whig interest will be unanswerable. . . .

Granted, then, that it was necessary to fix an uniform franchise for all the boroughs, what was the standard to be? The first decision of the Committee of Four was in favour of householders rated at £10. But on second thoughts, at Durham's suggestion and against Russell's wish, they inserted the Radical panacea of election by ballot, and as a make-weight altered the more popular £10 franchise to the more exclusive £20. Durham, who was closely in touch with outside opinion, believed that the ballot was so generally demanded by Reformers, that it must be included at any price to ensure Radical support for the Bill. But the price he proposed was too high; the £20 householders would have formed an oligarchy scarcely requiring the protection of the ballot. However, when the Committee's draft bill went up to the Cabinet in the middle of January, it contained the ballot and the £20 franchise. Grey and most of the Cabinet objected to the ballot, which was at once struck out. And after a month's uncertainty the more popular £10 franchise was restored. Russell, who was to introduce the Bill, produced at the last moment fresh calculations showing that the £20 franchise would yield a much more restricted electorate than the Cabinet ever intended to create; it would make so many new "rotten boroughs." Durham, Althorp, and Brougham were also strong advocates of the broader franchise, which was re-adopted just in time. Ten pounds and no ballot was after all the best policy, for the King declared that he would never have agreed to the ballot, and then people would never have been content with the twenty pounds.

Even the £10 franchise was none too generous; it did not include the whole middle class. . . . Only half of them had votes; and the redistribution of seats, enormous as it had been, was yet far from being complete, or just to the middle class. Though "nomination" boroughs were all gone, there were many small, corrupt boroughs left, over which the neighbouring gentry could exert great influence. The old borough-mongering oligarchy disappeared in 1832, but the landed gentry as a whole were the governing class until 1846, and even after the repeal of the Corn Laws they had immense power until the Reform Act of 1867. John Bright, in agitating for household suffrage in the 'sixties, thus summed up the electoral position:

The working men are almost universally excluded, roughly and insolently, from political power; and the middle class, whilst they have the semblance of it, are defrauded of the reality.

Bright used always to say of the First Reform Bill: "It was not a good Bill, but it was a great Bill when it passed." It was a great Bill because it passed — and by passing put an end to Burke's doctrine that the British constitution could not be altered with the changing years. A more perfect Bill, such as the experience of our later age could, doubtless, dictate, would have failed to pass in 1832, and its rejection would sooner or later have been followed by a civil war. . . .

In the last half of January 1831 the Cabinet discussed the proposals of the Committee of Four. Except for the ballot, there was singularly little opposition to the principles of the Bill, once Brougham's incipient rebellion against the total abolition of rotten boroughs had been firmly suppressed by Grey. Palmerston, Lansdowne, and Richmond, the chiefs of the "moderate" party, seem to have grumbled more against the Bill after it had been brought before the public, than during these preliminary counsels in the secrecy of the Cabinet. Like the King, they were persuaded by Grey, who had great influence over them all, to regard it as a conservative measure designed to save the threatened constitution and to put the question to rest. And like the King they were only gradually aroused to the enormity of what they were doing, by the unappeasable fury of the borough-mongers after the provisions of the Bill became known. At any rate it was only in April that Palmerston began appealing to Grey to modify the disfranchisement clauses. . . .

After the Bill had run the gauntlet of the Cabinet, Grey went down to Brighton on Sunday the 30th of January to unfold the measure to the King. It was potentially the most critical day in the whole history of Reform, for a refusal on the King's part to agree on some vital point must have led to a crisis, at a time when neither the Government nor their Bill had yet attained the consistency and popularity required if a crisis was to be faced. The resignation of the whole Cabinet, shaken by simultaneous failure on other questions, or a split between Brougham and the moderates on one side and Grey, Althorp, and Durham on the other, might easily have occurred if the King had exercised his admitted right of preliminary veto on the Bill. As it was, all went well. But he wrote to Grey four days later that if the ballot or universal suffrage had been in the Bill he would have refused permission to bring it in — a prohibition which Grey acknowledged as "a command he was bound to obey." Such was then the custom of the constitution. . . .

William was more easily courted, because his theory of constitutional propriety, the opposite of that of his father and brother before him, forbade him to listen to Tory advisers and favourites, so long as he had a Whig ministry. . . . This new reading of the constitutional duty of the sovereign to his Ministers was fostered in the King's mind by his private secretary Sir Herbert Taylor, a man of no political prejudices and great political instinct, to whom the British constitution owes much of its development along the paths of peace.

The King was prepared to hold the balance between Whigs and Tories, so long as each according to their rival methods helped him to defeat the "extravagant and mischievous projects" of the Radicals. His fixed idea that the Radicals wished to overset the throne, which made him suspect and dislike the uncompromising Durham in a manner only too apparent, was turned by Grey's more skilful management to the advantage of the Liberal cause. The Prime Minister persuaded the King that only a large measure of Reform could save the institutions of the country, especially the throne, from Radical assault. Ninety years have shown the substantial truth of this view, as contrasted with the Tory prophecy that if the Bill passed there would soon be "No King, no Lords, no inequalities in the social system; all will be levelled to the plane of petty shopkeepers and farmers; this not perhaps without bloodshed, but certainly by confiscations and persecutions." When the King called the Bill "an aristocratical measure," the Tories laughed bitterly and accused Grey of playing upon his simplicity. Yet in persuading the King that the Bill would save the throne and the aristocracy and prevent bloodshed, Grey spoke his own honest belief, which turned out to be correct.

There was, however, one aspect of the Bill which the King entirely misunderstood. He did not foresee that the "aristocratical measure" would be regarded as confiscation and revolution by the class and type of men with whom he himself had most natural affinity; still less that it would lead to a conflict between the two Houses of Parliament in which the People, whose inter-ference he dreaded and deprecated, would finally thrust him aside from the post of umpire and act in that usurped authority with an extreme vigour. Yet even on this point Grey did not deceive him. The King was deceived by his own simplicity and did not raise the question until it was too late.

And so, on the anniversary of the execution of Charles I, his so different successor consented to "the Bill, the whole Bill, and nothing but the Bill.". . . The month of February had still to roll away, bringing with it every sort of failure in Parliament and the country, while the popularity and prestige of the Ministry decreased daily. But Grey's spirits remained buoyant and serene, for he knew that he had a panacea for all these minor troubles. He had cut out, in front of his party's march, a clear path through that Reform jungle in which both friend and foe had expected to see him miserably entangled. Men who had known him too well as the hesitating and pessimistic leader of opposition, always trying to avoid responsibility and action, could not believe that he had stepped quietly forward and plucked the flower safely from the nettle danger. . . .

Whigs Were Aided by the Middle Class

G. LOWES DICKINSON

G. Lowes Dickinson (1862–1932), humanist, historian, and philosopher, wrote over a dozen books and many articles in his lifetime. The author of *Revolution and Reaction in Modern France* (1892), and *The European Anarchy, 1904–1914* (1926), Mr. Dickinson also wrote the *Development of Parliament During the Nineteenth Century* (1895), from which the following selection is taken. He argues that the Reform Act was not forced upon the aristocracy by the people, but was introduced by the Whig section of the aristocracy and carried against the Tory section with the support of the middle class.

During the course of the last sixty years a revolution has been effected in the government of England. The power has been transferred from the control of a compact and vigorous aristocracy to that of a democracy which in fact, though not in outward form, is more complete and more uncontrolled than any at present existing in any first-class State. So rapid has the transition been, and at the same time so quiet, that we have hardly realised that it has been taking place. There has been no violence, no overt change of principle; all that has been done has been done in the name, and under the forms, of the same constitution that supported a monarchy in the sixteenth and an aristocracy in the eighteenth century. Yet the transformation is fundamental, as we are just beginning to perceive. . . .

The first step in the transition of which we are to trace the course is the Reform Act of 1832. Because it was the first, it was the most vigorously opposed and therefore the most vigorously supported. But though it evoked in its defence a violent popular agitation, it was not forced upon the aristocracy by the people; it was deliberately and voluntarily introduced by one section of the governing class and carried by them against the other with the help of the populace. How then did it come about that a strong and capable aristocracy should have brought themselves to initiate a measure which has been shown, by the course of events, to have been nothing more or less than an abdication? Here is the starting-point of our historical inquiry.

The aristocracy of England in the eighteenth century occupied a peculiar position. While they were surpreme in fact, their supremacy was exercised under the forms of a constitution which contained, in theory at least, a popular element. The House of Commons, as we read in so conservative an authority as Blackstone, ought, if only it safely could, to have been elected freely by the votes of all citizens, however mean. "If it were probable," he says, "that every man could give his vote freely, and without influence of any kind, then upon the true theory and genuine principles of liberty, every member of the community, however poor, should have a vote in electing those delegates to whose charge is committed the disposal of his property, his liberty and his life." "This," he continues, with unconscious irony, "is the spirit of our constitution"; how far it was the practice is sufficiently notorious. The franchise was not

From G. Lowes Dickinson, *Development of Parliament during the Nineteenth Century* (London, 1895), Chapter I. Reprinted by permission of Longmans, Green & Company Ltd., and the executors, Estate of G. Lowes Dickinson.

only not universal, it was not regulated by any principle at all, whether of property, intelligence, or birth. In the counties it belonged to the 40s. freeholders; in the boroughs to one or other section of the inhabitants, here to the members of the corporation, here to the freeholders, here to the potwallopers, no rule for the privilege being discernible, and no intelligible end in its variety. Moreover, since the seventeenth century no new boroughs had been created, while many of the old ones had lost all importance, and some of them all but their parliamentary existence, so that the borough representation bore no proportion at all either to the wealth or the population of the country. "Seventy of your members," as it is pathetically remarked in a petition presented to parliament in 1793, "are returned by thirty-five places . . . in which it would be to trifle with the patience of your honourable house to mention any number of voters whatever, the elections at the places alluded to being notoriously a mere matter of form."

Such an arrangement of the franchise was as favourable to the power of the aristocracy as it was unfavourable to popular representation. In the counties the influence of the landed gentry was naturally supreme, by virtue at once of their economic position and their social prestige; but under the existing system it was further extended to the boroughs. The members returned to Parliament by "a green mound" or "a stone wall with three niches in it" were nominees of the gentlemen on whose estates these remains of former cities stood; the few insignificant electors of a little county town were not likely to oppose the will of the resident landlord; and, even if opposition were attempted, it was not difficult to meet it. Votes might be created, if necessary, by the division of freeholds; burgage tenants might be induced to sell under penalty of a worse fate; and when intimidation failed there was always the resource of bribery. The franchise, indeed, as often as not, was regarded by its possessors as a means of making money. Votes were known to

fetch as much as 100 £. apiece; 20 £. was not an uncommon average; and in the corporate towns it was noticed that as a general election approached the number of freemen would be suddenly increased owing to the pecuniary value of the vote. As the general result of the conditions we are not surprised to find that the majority of the boroughs were regarded as the property of certain proprietors, whose names are to be found printed in Oldfield's "Representative History"; that by these proprietors they were commonly sold for sums which ranged as high as 5,000 £. for a single parliament; and that advertisements appeared in the newspapers, of which the following may serve as a characteristic example: "A certain great assembly: 1,400 guineas per annum will be given for a seat in the above assembly."

This system, indeed, had one advantage, that it enabled independent men to buy their way into Parliament, and so escape the necessity of submitting to a patron; it was thus, for example, that Sir Samuel Romilly obtained his seat. But such cases were comparatively rare. The majority of the borough seats were filled by nominees of the aristocracy, and in this way members of the House of Lords practically controlled a considerable portion of the representation of the Commons. Of the six hundred and fifty-eight members of the Lower House it was calculated that not more than a hundred and seventy could be described as independent; the whole of the remainder were returned by patrons, and nearly one-half of the whole number by peers.

But of all the influences brought to bear upon the House of Commons, the most important was that of the minister in power. Not only did he control the representation of a large number of the boroughs, either by purchase or through the votes of government officials, but he was also in a position to bribe those who were not his nominees. This, indeed, was a recognized part of his business, and the usual mode of securing a majority. Representatives who had bought their seats expected a return for their money. . . . A place in parliament was a career, and one of the most lucrative of careers. The capital invested in the purchase of a seat returned a high percentage, and a pension or a sinecure, a profitable contract, or an interest in a public loan was the recognised reward of a vote conscientiously reserved for the minister in power. . . .

Such then, in brief, was the position of the aristocracy in the eighteenth century. Its weakness, it will be perceived, resided in two points. In the first place, the constitution, which in practice was the tool of a privileged class, in theory admitted a popular element. The House of Commons was supposed to be composed of representatives of the people; it was composed, in fact, of nominees of the aristocracy, introduced and controlled by open and avowed corruption. From this point of view the position was exposed to a double attack; on the one hand the theory was discrepant with the fact, on the other the discrepancy was maintained by a gross and notorious abuse of influence.

In the second place the very machinery which made possible the predominance of the aristocracy in the lower house made possible also the independence of the executive. By influence, direct or indirect, at the elections or in the house, the minister could buy a majority. But behind the minister stood the crown; and a strong or an obstinate sovereign, as was shown in the case of George III, might initiate and carry through a disastrous policy, in defiance of the opposition not only of the people but of the governing class. Here, then, was an internal contradiction in the system; by the very means which they employed to govern, the aristocracy lost the power of government; and, as we shall see, it was through the dread of an administrative despotism that they were driven into the path of reform.

For reform, as we have said, proceeded from the ranks of the aristocracy itself, and to this is to be attributed the particular shape it assumed. The explanation of the provisions of the Reform Act of 1832 lies in the character of Whig opinion; and it is

to this topic that we must now address ourselves.

The modern man, looking back over the system that has just been described, has no difficulty in recognising the necessity of reform. But that is because he is unconsciously imbued with the democratic ideal, and makes assumptions which would never have been admitted by an aristocrat of the eighteenth century. He assumes that representation of the people means the representation of numbers; but that is precisely what was denied by every section of the aristocracy. Whigs as well as Tories were emphatic in their repudiation of the whole theory of democracy, either as an ideal for the future or as the tradition of the past. . . . On this point, at least, the whole governing class was at one, that representation of the people did not and ought not to imply the representation of numerical preponderance.

On the other hand they believed that, in a certain sense, the House of Commons did represent the people. It represented, in their view, the various interests of the country; and this, they thought, it was enabled to do by virtue of that very constitution which the modern man condemns without a hearing. It was precisely, they affirmed, because the franchise was unequally and capriciously distributed that the House of Commons was a real epitome of the nation. Under a system of universal suffrage every section of the people in a minority would be deprived of political existence; under the system in force there was no section, however small, that had not a chance of sending a member to parliament. . . . And while on the one hand the system was elastic enough to admit of these superficial variations, on the other it was broadly based on the two great interests of the country, that of the land, represented by the counties and the smaller towns, and that of commerce, represented by such cities as London and Liverpool.

Such is the view of the constitution which was constantly upheld by the aristocracy against the various propositions of reform. . . . Nor was the theory confined to those who opposed reform; it is substantially accepted by Lord John Russell in his "Essay on the History of the English Government and Constitution," and reappears, as we shall see, in the utterances of both Liberals and Conservatives for years after the date of the first Reform Act. . . .

The House of Commons then, upon the aristocratic view, was not, and never had been intended to be, a sort of arithmetical machine for counting heads; and, upon the same principle, its members were not conceived as mere symbols of such and such a quantitative value. A member was not a delegate; he was a representative. "This House," said Sir Robert Inglis in 1832, "is not a collection of deputies, as the States-General of Holland and as the assemblies in some other continental countries. We are not sent here day by day to represent the opinions of our constituents. Their local rights, their municipal privileges we are bound to protect; their general interests we are bound to consult at all times; but not their will, unless it shall coincide with our own deliberate sense of right." It followed that, even supposing the House of Commons should find itself for a time in opposition to the people, this was not necessarily either a contradiction or an evil. It proceeded, naturally enough, from the true theory of the constitution, and might well be an advantage rather than the reverse. . . .

So far we have been considering the view held by the aristocracy of the relation of the House of Commons to the people; but the Commons had a further relation to the other branches of the Government, to the Crown and to the House of Lords. And here, too, what appeared as an anomaly, when considered by itself and apart, was regarded as necessary and normal, when considered in its relation to the whole. The influence of the Crown and of the Peers in the elections to the Commons would, indeed, have been an absurdity had the latter been supposed to be an independent body. But, in fact, it was not; it was one member of a trinity; and its partial determination by the other factors in the scheme was pre-cisely the condition of harmony between what would otherwise have been conflicting and discordant powers. . . .

The theory which has thus been briefly analysed was that held by all sections of the governing class, and it was only within its limits that the divergence on the question of reform came in. To Tories, on the one hand, the system, exactly as it was, was as good as a system possibly could be; it was "our present happy constitution — the happiest, the best, and the most noble constitution of the world, and I do not believe it possible to make it better." Any change must be a change for the worse, nay, it must be the prelude to a radical subversion, for there was no principle authorising reform which would not also authorise revolution. Even Canning here is substantially at one with the rank and file of the party. "If this House," he says, "is not all that we could wish it, I would rather rest satisfied with its present state than, by endeavouring to remedy some small defects, run the hazard of losing so much that is excellent." And this attitude of the Tories was also that of one school of the Whigs. Burke, on this point, may be classed with Wellington and Peel. For though he admitted, it is true, that if ever the time should come when the people should really be set upon reform, it would then be necessary to concede it, yet, clearly, he considered such a contingency to be as improbable as it would be disastrous. Of administrative reform, within the limits of the established system, he was an avowed and active champion; but to any alteration in the franchise he was consistently opposed. "Our representation," he said, "has been found perfectly adequate to all the purposes for which a representation of the people can be desired or devised. I defy the enemies of our constitution to show the contrary." And so profoundly was he convinced not only of the perfection but of the finality of the institutions of his time, that he does not hesitate to add: "We are resolved to keep an established church, an established monarchy, an established aristocracy, and an established democracy, each in the degree it exists, and in no greater."

But, on the other hand, there was another school of Whgs who, without impugning the general theory of the constitution, yet conceived that it might be possible and even necessary to modify it in detail. Institutions, in their view, must change with the change of circumstances; such had, in fact, been the maxim of the past, and they were the true Conservatives who applied it to the present. "The greatest innovation," according to Fox, "that could be introduced in the constitution of England, was to come to a vote that there should be no innovation in it. The greatest beauty of the constitution was, that in its very principle it admitted of perpetual improvement, which time and circumstances rendered necessary. It was a constitution, the chief excellence of which was that of admitting a perpetual reform" (1792).

To Whigs who examined from this point of view the practical working of the constitution, it apppeared, not indeed that its structure was vicious or unsound, but that in the course of time it had developed certain definite abuses which admitted of equally definite remedies. The evil as it was analysed by the Whig reformers centered about one point, the influence of the crown and the ministry. It was during the latter years of the American war that this abuse began to make itself felt. The war, in its later development, was at once unpopular and calamitous; it was continued, against the clear sense of the nation, by the personal influence of the king, exercised through the minister and his bought majority; and it ended in the loss of the American colonies. These were the facts that gave rise to the reform agitation of 1780. The executive had been clearly at variance with the nation, and equally clearly it had been wrong. Attention was naturally drawn to the conditions that made possible such a disaster, and they were found to depend upon the influence of the crown on the Commons. As Pitt put it in 1782: "The disastrous consequences of the American war, the immense expenditure of the public money, the consequent heavy burden of taxes, and the pressure of all the collateral difficulties produced by the foregoing circumstances gradually disgusted the people, and at last provoked them to 'turn their eyes inward on themselves,' in order to see if there was not something radically wrong at home. That was the chief cause of all the evils they felt from their misfortunes abroad." The result was the "county movement" of 1779 and 1780, which issued in the abortive motion introduced by Pitt to abolish the representation of certain of the smaller boroughs and transfer it to the more independent county electorate.

The American war was the clearest and most palpable example of the consequences to be feared from the personal influence of the Crown, but from that time onward the question was never dropped. In the circumstances of the great French war Fox imagined that he saw a repetition of those of the war with America; in both he maintained that a contest which was unpopular and unjust had been perpetrated against the declared sense of the nation by the corrupt influence of the minister in power; and in 1797 he supported the cause of reform against Pitt, on precisely the same grounds that had been advanced by Pitt himself in 1783.

After the peace, the same point of view recurs. The disturbed state of the country, from 1815 on, provoked the government to drastic measures. The Habeas Corpus Act was suspended, and the right of free speech and of public meeting practically suppressed. Once more it was felt that the liberties of the subject were not safe, that the government was approximating to an irresponsible tyranny; and Lord John Russell, writing in 1823, is so far from anticipating the advent of democracy that he professes to fear the extinction of the constitution in a despotism. . . .

It seems clear, then, that it was dread of the influence of the sovereign and his ministers that was the main motive swaying the Whigs to reform. But that influence was exercised mainly through the medium of the smaller boroughs. These were the seats that were open to purchase, and for which such members were returned as were ready to sell themselves to the government. It was observed that every attempt to introduce retrenchment or reform was defeated by a solid phalanx of borough members. They, then, were the root of every public evil, of disastrous expeditions, of extravagant finance, of the debt, the increased taxation, and the consequent disturbance and distress. It followed that if the control of the executive was the object of the Whigs, the means to that control was a reform in the machinery of representation.

Of this attitude of the Whigs the Act of 1832 is the clearest record and exponent. Its object was to disfranchise all the boroughs which were most obviously open to sinister influences, and by transferring the seats thus gained to the counties and the larger towns to replace the nominees of a Tory government by members of more independent, perhaps of more whiggish views. But never for one moment did the Whig ministry intend to alter the essential character of the House. In the changes they introduced they were bound, it is true, to be guided to some extent by considerations of property and numbers. But, as they were careful to explain, it was never their idea to accept either wealth or population as a sole and sufficient basis of representation; "wealth, probity, learning, and wit" are all to be considered; more than one hundred seats are still preserved to the smaller boroughs, to represent the general interest of the nation against the particular interests of localities; the supremacy of the landed interest is to be maintained; the influence of the peers, if anything, is to be increased; and the balance of the powers in the constitution is to be maintained.

Whether we consider, therefore, the theory held by the aristocracy as a whole, or the particular modification of it which prompted the Reform Act of the Whigs, it is clear that that Act was never intended by the governing class either to be or to lead to a fundamental change in the constitution of the House of Commons; it was not directed primarily against inequality of representation as such, but against certain specific abuses which were supposed to have resulted incidentally therefrom, and especially against the increasing influence of the Crown and the ministry.

But the views and the intentions of the aristocracy were but one factor in the situation. For though it was the Whigs who introduced the Bill, it was popular agitation from without that carried it through. No measure that has ever been introduced, from that day to this, has excited an enthusiasm in any way comparable to that of 1832; and there can be little doubt that, unless the House of Lords had been forced to yield, violent revolution would have ensued. As it was, the agitation was pushed to the extreme limit of legality — the Commons were petitioned to withhold supplies; the public were invited to refuse taxes, and to paralyse industry by a run upon the banks; and, as a last resort, a plan of armed insurrection had actually been made out. Such a popular upheaval, it might well be supposed, must be more significant of the real opinion of the nation than the wishes and hopes of the aristocracy; and it therefore becomes important to consider what the agitation really meant, and whether, or to what extent, it was based on democratic ideas.

One thing is clear to begin with. Whatever else the movement may have implied, it reflected, at any rate, an intense dissatisfaction with things as they were. This can be traced from the closing years of the eighteenth century, and may be referred to two main causes — the first, a general feeling of injustice in the exclusive predominance of a privileged class; the second, a yet keener sense of immediate practical grievances.

The jealousy and mistrust on the part of those who are excluded from power, which is the nemesis of all class government, was exaggerated in the particular case with which we are concerned by the belief that the government was also a usurpation. . . .

The result was an indictment, which may be briefly summarised as follows: — The aristocracy are a sort of joint-stock company, exploiting the nation for their own ends by the most questionable and discreditable means; the House of Commons is their instrument, stocked with the creatures of their will — "idle schoolboys, insignificant coxcombs, led-captains and toad-eaters, profligates, gamblers, bankrupts, beggars, contractors, commissaries, public plunderers, ministerial dependents, hirelings and wretches that would sell their country or deny their God for a guinea." Working through such tools as these, the aristocracy have absolute control of the finance and the policy of the nation. Of this finance, the whole end and aim is to extort money from the poor in order to distribute it among the rich — "to draw money," as Bentham puts it, "out of the pockets of the blinded, deluded, unsuspicious, uninquisitive, and ever too patient people," and to bestow it in the form of pensions and sinecures upon their own dependents and relatives. Parliament may, therefore, appropriately be styled the "taxing thing," and its members the "tax-eating crew." In the performance of this important function the one object they keep in view is the maximum oppression of the people and the minimum inconvenience to the governing class. Land is, therefore, tenderly treated, for land is the property of the aristocracy; so are country mansions, for in them the aristocracy live; an income-tax is avoided, for to it the aristocracy must contribute, or, if it is imposed, it is abolished again on the first opportunity. Meantime, for the starving labourer not a single necessity is spared; he pays on his beer, his shoes, his candles, his soap, his tea, and his meat; his bread is raised to a famine price by the protective duties on corn, whose only object is to increase the rent that goes into the landlord's pocket; and if, in his distress, he is driven to kill a pheasant or a hare, he is hauled before a magistrate, who is also the owner of the game, and at a third offence may be transported for seven years.

While such was the typical reformer's view of the domestic operations of the government, he was not less severe on their foreign policy. Here, too, he detected the same sordid ends and the same discreditable means. Did the aristocracy make war, it was to find pay for the army chiefs, or to suppress liberty abroad for fear it should assert itself at home. Did they found colonies, it was for the sake of the lucrative governorships. Did they maintain a peace establishment, it was to secure and perpetuate their own ascendency. . . . And so with all their wars, with all their conquests and colonisations — one end, and one alone, has directed the whole conspiracy, to secure the position of the governing class, and to fill their pockets with gold. National honour? National duty? National necessity? Pshaw! These are the cloaks and disguises, the cunning machinery of fraud! . . .

Enough has been said to indicate the general point of view from which the aristocracy was regarded by reformers of the middle class, and to account for the fierceness and vigour of the agitation of 1832. But to hate an aristocracy is not the same thing as to love a democracy; and it still remains for us to inquire whether this revolt against the governing class was prompted exclusively by practical grievances, or whether it had also a theoretic basis in a democratic conception of the State.

The democratic theory had, in fact, been advanced from the very beginning of the movement for reform. . . . Nor can it be said that these ideas were confined to individual thinkers, and were never made known outside a narrow circle. Major Cartwright was an active and able agitator, and was a main agent in the formation of the Hampden Clubs, which sprang up at the beginning of the century. The influence of Paine may be traced in the London Corresponding Society (1792), which was composed mainly of artisans, and of which we are told that "a great majority of the members were Republicans." Bentham was more influential in law than in politics; but he was the friend and teacher of James Mill and of Francis Place, and it was he who drew up the motion for reform brought forward by Burdett in 1818. The democratic view, it may be said, was fairly before the country. Was it the view which the country chose to adopt?

In answering this question it is necessary to draw a broad distinction between the position of the middle and that of the working class. The leaders of the working class, as we shall notice more particularly in a later chapter, were from the first suspicious of the Reform Bill of the Whigs. It was with reluctance that they consented to connect themselves with the agitation at all; in so far as they did so, it was only from the point of view that the measure, though of little value in itself, was at least a step in the direction of what they wanted; and after it was passed they proceeded at once, with perfect consistency, to agitate for a new and more radical reform. The real supporters of the Bill of 1832 were the middle class, and they supported it frankly for what it was and not for what they hoped it would lead to. The Bill gave them the franchise, and it was the franchise that they wanted. Even those of them who professed to the full the principle of government by the people, were really thinking of government by themselves. . . . But there is no reason to suppose that the mass of the middle class were desirous of a wider extension of the franchise, even with the assurance that it would only enhance their own supremacy. On the contrary, it seems clear that they did genuinely accept the Bill of the Whigs as sufficient and as final. For, in the first place, they actively opposed the later Chartist agitation, the programme of which was frankly democratic; in the second place, they were so far from being anxious to disturb the new order of things that, as we shall see, it would be truer to say that further reform was forced upon the country by the government than that it was forced upon the government by the country.

Nor is this attitude difficult to understand. If we look behind the rhetoric in which reformers of the middle class were wont to denounce a corrupt and tyrannical oligarchy, we shall find, as a rule, not any complete and *a priori* theory of democracy, but merely a keen sense of certain specific grievances, similar in kind, though felt with a more intense and bitter rancour, to those which were denounced by the Whigs of the governing class. Cobbett, for example, the most able and the most influential of all the reformers, is by no means a democrat in principle. Not only does he believe in the Crown and in the House of Lords, but he disbelieves in universal suffrage. . . . On the other hand, he does believe in a reform of parliament, because there are evils which he wants to see redressed. With extraordinary vigour and pertinacity he expresses what was at bottom the real complaint of the middle class: that they had not sufficient control over the raising and expenditure of the public funds; that an enormous debt had been contracted in the prosecution of wars which had been initiated and persevered in against the nation's will; that in the incidence of taxation favour was shown to the landed interest at the expense of all the other classes of the population; that the peace establishment maintained after 1815 was disproportionately large, and that this, together with the interest of the debt, and the payment in salaries, pensions, and sinecures, constituted an intolerable burden on the people's industry. . . .

It was, in fact, the burden of taxation that gave body and form to that general mistrust and hatred of the aristocracy to which we have already referred. But this was an evil that would be met, it might be supposed, so far as the middle class was concerned, by the action of the Bill of 1832. By that measure the middle class were admitted to the franchise; they would exercise henceforth an important influence on the Lower House, and would have the redress of their grievances in their own hands. There was no reason why they should wish for anything more, and it is clear, I think, that as a body they did not. "The Bill, the whole Bill, and nothing but the Bill" was a formula of conviction, not merely of expediency. Substantially, by the Act of 1832, the middle class got what they wanted, and of this their hostility to Chartism and their indifference to further measures of reform are a sufficient and conclusive proof.

From the whole of this investigation results the following conclusion. Neither the Whig aristocracy who introduced the first Reform Bill, nor the middle class whose agitation forced it through, conceived it to be, even implicitly, a revolutionary measure. The power of the Crown and the House of Lords were to be maintained intact; the House of Commons was to be more representative, but not more democratic, than before. The change was regarded as one of detail, not one of principle; in no sense a subversion of the constitution, but merely its adaptation to new conditions.

Theories, it is true, had been broached which led straight to pure democracy, and these, no doubt, were producing their effect; but it was not they that carried the Act of 1832. . . . The agitation of 1832 was a movement of the middle class, and it was genuinely set upon that particular measure without ulterior democratic ends. Here the middle class were at one with the Whig aristocracy; the idea of both was to reform the constitution, not to transform it. But the expectation of both has been falsified by the irony of history. Reform has been found to be only another name for transformation; and the Bill of 1832, so far from being final, has proved to be but the first step in an irresistible process towards democracy.

II. CAUSES OF THE REFORM BILL: SOME MODERN AND SOME CONTEMPORARY VIEWS

Reform Not Affected by the French Revolution

NORMAN GASH

Norman Gash (born 1912) is professor of history at St. Andrew's University, Scotland. The author of three recent works, *Mr. Secretary Peel* (1961), *Politics in the Age of Peel* (1953), and *Reaction and Reconstruction in English Politics, 1832–1852* (1965) (the Ford Lectures of 1964), Gash has also written an important article on Peel and the party system. In this article he concludes that, while it may have affected the rhetoric of the Radicals, the French Revolution had little impact upon a number of contested elections in the general election of 1830.

THE VIEW THAT the English general election of 1830 was strongly and sympathetically affected by the July revolution in France is one that has never been seriously challenged even though it has not always been wholeheartedly accepted. One of the most authoritative exponents of this opinion was Halévy. In his *History of the English People* he stated that the news of the events in France, coming when the borough elections had just started and the county elections were about to begin, "provoked in England an indescribable storm of popular feeling which swept the country and was most unfavourable to the government." But Halévy was basing himself on much contemporary assertion. One of the tory contentions in the Reform Bill debates was that Grey's ministry had only come into power because of the artificial excitement caused by the French Revolution. The strongly conservative *Annual Register* in its review of the year argued that as a result of the events in France "the general election took place in a period of greater public excitation, directed towards great changes in the frame of the government, than had occurred since the period of the French Revolution," and added that in no popular election did any candidate find himself a gainer by announcing himself as an adherent of the Government. Wellington himself attributed to that excitement the major responsibility for his parliamentary defeat in November 1830. "The administration was beaten by two events," he wrote at the end of December. "First, the Roman Catholic question; next, the French Revolution." But though he admitted that over Catholic Emancipation "we estranged our own party," he thought the ministry would still have been too strong for the whigs, "if the

From Norman Gash, "English Reform and French Revolution in the General Election of 1830," in Richard Pares and A. J. P. Taylor, eds., *Essays Presented to Sir Lewis Namier* (London, 1956), pp. 258–273, 287–288. Reprinted by permission of St. Martin's Press, Inc., The Macmillan Company of Canada Ltd., and Macmillan & Co. Ltd.

French Revolution had not occurred at the very moment of the dissolution of Parliament." . . .

Wellington, before his parliamentary defeat, showed no awareness that the general election had made it impossible for his ministry to continue. At the beginning of September he told Vesey Fitzgerald that what the government lacked was not numbers in the House of Commons but talent in the cabinet. . . . In this mood of mild optimism he was not peculiar. To few people did the result of the general election seem at the time to clarify what was admittedly a confused political situation. If the ultra-tory *Standard* announced that the result would be the formation of a strong "country" party, the whig *Morning Chronicle* talked with confidence of the overthrow of the squirearchy at the recent elections. On two points only was there general agreement: that the government had been neither influential nor popular; and that there would be a strong movement for enquiry, retrenchment and reform in the new session. Party men in government and Opposition made the conventional claims to have gained on balance from the elections. But nice statistics of this kind were almost irrelevant. Neither before nor after the election did the government command a majority in the House of Commons. Even when Wellington was writing to Fitzgerald, the Treasury whips were calculating that less than a half of the House could be reckoned as firm supporters. This, of course, did not necessarily spell doom to the ministry. The House was not based on a rigid two-party system and the organized body of the Opposition numbered less than two hundred. In these circumstances, though the position of the government was not easy, there was at least room for manoeuvre. The question posed by the 1830 election was not whether the government had lost outright control of the House of Commons, but whether the character and temper of the new House would deprive the government of its ability to manoeuvre successfully any longer.

It was privately admitted by the ministerialists during the autumn that they could not hope to stay in office without a reinforcement of "speaking talent" in the Commons. But, when it came to the point, no reinforcement was available except on condition of parliamentary reform. It was true that when the ministers abruptly resigned in November 1830, it was on another issue; but they did so to evade the question of reform and to put responsibility for that subject on their successors. Whatever Grey's personal feelings were on taking office, parliamentary reform was an inescapable legacy left to him by the outgoing government. The subject on which men soon began to differ, however, was whether this irresistible demand for reform was simply the culmination of a long domestic agitation, or the fortuitous result of a coincidence during the summer of an English general election with a French revolution.

The chronological coincidence was, in fact, rather finer than is generally realized. On 28 July *The Times* reported the promulgation of the Polignac ordinances. On 2 August came the news of rioting in Paris and republican successes; and on 3 August the English newspapers were able to give detailed accounts of the fighting and announce the formation of the provisional Government. By that date, most of the English elections were already over. In many constituencies electoral activity had started in early July and by the middle of the month candidates were taking the field all over the country. By 29 July the first elections had started and by 3 August *The Times* could report the results in over sixty constituencies and the return of over 120 members. The difference between the timing of the county and borough elections was not quite so uniform or distinct as Halévy suggested; but in general the elections in the uncontested English boroughs were decided in the last two days of July and the first two days of August; the counties and most of the contested boroughs in the first week or ten days of August.

Yet how many elections were actually

contested in 1830? Even in the twenty years after the Reform Act the average number of constituencies contested at a general election was only just over half. Before the Reform Act the proportion was undoubtedly smaller, even though exact statistics are hard to obtain. H. S. Smith, in his *Contested Elections* (1842), records only sixty-one contests in England and Wales at the general election of 1830. As he ignored the fifty-six rotten boroughs disfranchised in 1832 the real figure is slightly higher. But of those omitted constituencies only eight were contested in 1830, and only one of them (Stockbridge, Hants) made its return after 2 August. Even allowing for the omissions and possible defects in Smith's compilation, it is probable that little more than a quarter of the 269 English and Welsh constituencies were contested in 1830. It is true that uncontested elections frequently concealed a decision of some sort, and might even reflect a measure of public opinion. But it would necessarily be a decision taken some days, perhaps weeks, earlier and not likely therefore to be influenced by sudden extraneous events at the time of the election itself. But even with the contested elections, the real consideration is whether they were decided after the news of the successful July revolution had reached the English public through the morning newspapers on 3 August. . . . Of the sixty-one contests listed by Smith, twenty-six were already decided by 2 August. His figures must, as already indicated, be scaled up slightly. But as all but one of the contested boroughs he omitted to consider concluded their elections before 3 August, the revised total is only thirty-six. Exact figures are impossible until the whole election is subjected to large-scale research. Yet the tentative conclusion must be that probably less than forty contested constituencies in England and Wales were decided after 2 August. If so, the amount of voting open to the direct impact of the July revolution was considerably restricted.

It would be wrong, of course, to take into account merely the actual votes cast after that critical date. Atmosphere and emotion are important in politics though they are not easily translatable into statistics. Even candidates certain of their seat might be infected by popular enthusiasms or impressed by strong views among their constituents at the time of their election. Of the intense interest roused by the news from France there can be no doubt. It started not merely with the Paris riots or the Polignac ordinances but with the elections to the new French Chamber early in July. At the beginning of the month there were press comments on the probable course of the elections in France and on 9 July *The Times* had a leader on the political problems facing Charles X. French internal politics continued to occupy a large share of the foreign news and between 20 and 23 July *The Times* devoted its chief leading article almost daily to the French situation. Once the revolution broke out, both the national and the provincial press gave extremely full reports; and up to the end of August, *The Times* at least continued to make a feature of French news. Indeed, while providing its readers with a steady flow of report and comment on affairs in France, the newspaper curiously omitted to give any general review of the results of the general election in England.

The issue, however, is not whether the British reading public took a marked interest in the revolutionary proceedings in France at this date, but whether they were prepared to draw analogies between the contemporary situation in the two countries or to derive inspiration from abroad for a forward movement at home. Some undoubtedly were; and it is perhaps symptomatic that the most important of these were drawn from the extreme wings of English politics — the ultra-radicals and the ultra-tories. . . .

With the outbreak of the revolution in Paris, the French analogy became a feature of lower-class Radical propaganda. Hume, appearing for the first time as prospective member for Middlesex in an unopposed election, told the crowd on nomination day (5 August) that if they needed an example, a glorious one might be found in a neighbouring state; and though he had too high an opinion of his country to think that the occasion would ever arrive for such proceedings as had lately taken place in France, he hoped the people of England would be as sensible of their rights as the people of France. Cobbett in his *Political Register* contended that the effect of the French revolution must be to hasten reform in England, and in a series of speeches and lectures in the late summer and autumn proceeded to ram home the point with his usual vigorous and repetitive technique. . . . Between 9 September and 7 October he delivered a set of eleven lectures on "The French and Belgian Revolutions and English Boroughmongering" at the Rotunda in Blackfriars Road. But two factors limited the effect of Cobbett's arguments. . . . The people in whose minds his arguments found readiest approval were for the most part the poorer, unenfranchised classes who at most could only have an indirect influence on the elections. In the second place, his propaganda developed its main strength after and not during the elections. . . . If the July revolution presented a lesson to the British public, it was one that required at least a few days for absorption. In fact, it was not until the elections were largely over that the Radical spokesmen began generally to elaborate the analogy of French revolution and English reform. From their point of view it would have been better had the events in Paris preceded rather than accompanied the English elections. The coincidence was a little too exact. . . .

The Government undoubtedly took the signs of revolutionary contagion seriously, but what they feared was not an alteration in the parliamentary balance of power but a direct threat to law and order, particularly in the northern industrial districts. "The success of the Mobs," wrote Peel, the home secretary, in the middle of October, "and either the unwillingness or inability of the soldiers to cope with them in Paris and Brussels, is producing its natural effect in the Manufacturing districts here, calling into action the almost forgotten Radicals of 1817 and 1819, and provoking a discussion upon the probable results of insurrectionary movements in this country." There were rumours of plots to seize the arms depot at Carlisle and a more credible account of the disturbed and ominous situation in Manchester, where the master manufacturers, like the troops in France and Belgium, seemed unwilling or unable to combine in self-defence. At the end of October there were several cabinet discussions on the dangerous state of the country, and simultaneously came reports of the serious disorders in Kent which heralded the widespread rioting among the country labourers of the south of England the following month. These disturbances, however, formed an administrative rather than a political problem and came after, not during, the general election.

It was left to the ultra-tories, from their superior station in the political world, to make more timely use of the French revolution. Not only were they themselves in a state of profound discontent with their own government, but the anti-clerical character of the July revolution was in their eyes an immediate recommendation for an event which in a more normal state of mind they might have regarded very differently. Obsessed as they were by the dangers of Catholicism, they ignored the aberration of political principle involved in their support for revolution. Nevertheless their tactics were shallow and patently opportunist, and it is questionable whether they were approved by more than a minority even among the general conservative elements in the country. Their propaganda scarcely convinced themselves; it did not convince many others. In essence their campaign was a continuation of the vendetta against Wellington and Peel that had started the previous year with the Government's decision to grant Catholic Emancipation. From that date Wellington in particular had become the target for ultra-tory abuse. Indeed, on the eve of the general election it was remarked that if the Government was not outstandingly popular, it was not strongly opposed on matters of policy by any section in parliament except the ultra-tories. The unrelenting hostility of that group was characteristically shown at the end of July when the *Standard* greeted the news of the Polignac ordinances with the ironic enquiry whether things were any better in England, and whether, if the French legislature was in as bad a state as the English, there would be much loss in its dissolution. With the outbreak of the revolution in Paris, however, the *Standard* recovered from this false start, went over to the popular side, and tried instead to damage Wellington's position by identifying him with the party of reaction in France. In the worst journalistic style it first, on 2 August, hinted at Wellington's complicity with Polignac, and then, the following day, demanded that Wellington should publicly deny the charge or else resign. A few days later Sir Richard Vyvyan, one of the more unbalanced of the ultra-tory country members, took up the running. At the Cornish county election meeting at Bodmin on 6 August, he delivered a rambling and, at times, almost unintelligible speech, in the course of which he compared Peel's metropolitan police with the French gendarmerie and Wellington with James II. The purpose of his oratory, however, was clear enough. He called on all parties to join in an "anti-Wellington party"; he argued that Catholic Emancipation was not an isolated question but part of a general struggle in Europe between Liberalism and representative government on the one side, tyranny and despotism on the other; and he spoke of the evident connexion between Wellington's actions and the ordinances of Polignac. The *Standard* immediately exploited this new ally, and for the rest of August and into September continued to insinuate that the prime minister had been an accomplice of the fallen and discredited French Government.

The fact remained, however, that scarcely a person of consequence was found to believe the charge. From the outset *The Times* championed the government on this issue and dismissed the story as the invention of a stupid and malignant faction. The *Morning Chronicle,* the chief Liberal organ, also defended Wellington, though in more lukewarm fashion, against this particular calumny. An excess of generosity was not to be expected from political opponents, but the whig Liberal party as a body preferred to leave the Polignac legend as the monopoly of the *Standard* and the rest of the ultra-tory press. . . . Whatever Wellington's faults were as a politician, no sensible person could have thought him an accomplice to the reactionary policy of the French Government. The British public of all classes and opinions condemned the French king and his ministers, and approved the July revolution; they had little reason to believe that their own Government did not share those sentiments.

United as Englishmen were in welcoming the revolution, however, they were not necessarily conscious of any need to extract from the scenes enacted in France a lesson for their own political behaviour. Indeed, the comments passed in the press and in public speeches on the French revolution are more characteristic of a mature and stable political society than of a country ripe for rebellion. The analogy that presented itself most strongly to the ordinary English mind was between 1830 and 1688. What England had achieved a century and a half ago, France was now after a long interval endeavouring to emulate. Hobhouse, the Radical, speaking from the hustings at the Middlesex election, declared that the heroic exertions of the French had rendered them worthy of obtaining what England had struggled to secure at her own revolution, a free press and a free parliament, and adjured the crowd to look upon the French as brothers. . . . The analogy between 1830 and 1688, which rapidly became a stock theme in the national press, was echoed in the counties. The *Leeds*

Mercury, one of the most influential of the provincial newspapers, used the comparison to refute the agitation of the ultra-radicals. To admire the French revolution and call for a similar change in England, it observed, was to show a profundity of ignorance. "Why, we had *our* 'Glorious Revolution' a hundred and forty years ago." France was only copying our example and imitating our institutions. Why should Englishmen play the monkey trick of "mimicking those who are imitating us"?

Englishmen of moderate views (and in 1830 they probably constituted the bulk of the electorate) were prepared to admit defects in their constitution and wished to have them reformed; but they could not see that there was any essential similarity between the political situation in France and in England. . . .

There was therefore perhaps less connexion in men's minds between the French revolution and the general election than might otherwise be supposed. In any case, however, the reform question had already been taking on a new significance before the election and, even without the continental disturbances, would probably have become a major issue in the new parliament. The reasons for this are not hard to find. For over twenty years Catholic Emancipation had overshadowed all other domestic controversies in British politics. Now that debate had ended, and at the same time the manner of its ending had deeply divided the party in politics which stood for a "conservation" of the existing constitution. Not only was the way clear for parliamentary reform to move into the front rank of active parliamentary issues, but some of the ultra-protestant tories had been driven by their exasperation and sense of impotence to look favourably on suggestions for a change in the structure of a legislature which they had patently ceased to control. The 1830 session had seen three plans for parliamentary reform put forward from different parts of the House, and though at the start of the year there had been signs of a whig alliance with the Government, the failure of Grey and Althorp to secure a postponement of the dissolution in July left the whig leaders in a hostile mood when the elections began. Even the *Annual Register* admitted that the spirit of opposition was at work in all quarters before Polignac issued his ill-fated ordinances the other side of the Channel. Reform perhaps would have been a better word than opposition. *The Times,* which was far from being anti-Governmental, suggested on 12 July a threefold test for electoral candidates: repeal of the Corn Laws, economical reform and the establishment of parliamentary representation for great and populous towns. The *Examiner* selected the same three topics — cheap bread, economy and parliamentary reform — as the issues of the day; and this diagnosis was quoted with the inference of agreement by the tory *Standard.* . . .

For professed parliamentary reformers to agitate for parliamentary reform was perhaps not in itself very remarkable. Of more significance was the deliberate agitation given to the question by the influential whig *Morning Chronicle.* The French elections earlier in July had already provided an occasion for a discussion in *The Times,* the *Globe* and the *Westminster Review,* among others, of the representative system in England; and the *Chronicle* in three succesive numbers devoted a leading article to a comparison of the British and French electoral systems and an exhaustive review of the issues raised in the general press discussion of parliamentary reform. Further leaders on the same topic appeared almost daily as the election drew nearer. Consistent encouragement was given to the reform movement in the country at large, including even guarded support for the ballot. The Reform Association's activities received its blessing; Brougham's candidature for Yorkshire was approved; and Cobbett himself received favourable mention. On 20 July, in a burst of feeling, the newspaper expressed the hope that the triumphs of Liberalism in the French elections would make the people of England "ashamed of the beastly orgies" of their own. What was most impressive in the *Chronicle's* prolonged campaign, however, was not an attempt to rouse a factitious excitement but its cool and realistic analysis of the actual defects and characteristics of the existing system: the decline in Government influence, the silent change in the electoral structure resulting from the greater diffusion of wealth and growing respectability of the electoral classes; venality in borough, subservience in county constituencies; the crippling expense of contested elections and its effect on the supply and character of candidates. All this, moreover, was being reiterated to its readers day after day for almost a month before the elections started.

In the end, of course, what counted was not what the newspapers said but how electors and candidates behaved. If the question is, how far the general election was influenced by the July revolution and how far that influence worked against the Government and in favour of reform, the answer must ultimately be sought in the elections themselves. . . .

Evidence from a limited number of elections is necessarily of itself limited. But incomplete as it is, it must at least cast some doubt on much of the generalized comment on the 1830 election that has passed into print. Seen in detail, the most striking feature of these individual elections is the importance of local and personal factors, and of domestic issues, rather than any signs of external stimulus. Government was weak but it is not true that opposition to Government was the only passport to electoral favour; and there was perhaps more respect for Wellington and Peel than has been commonly thought. Traditional party divisions existed but there were no clear party policies, and candidates came to terms as best they could with the electorate. The scene is at once more complicated and more human than the artificially simplified version offered later by observers after the

event. In most constituencies the elections probably followed a familiar pattern, and if the news of the revolution brought an additional excitement, it was of a vague and diffused kind. What could not be doubted was that many electors wanted reform of some sort or another — parliamentary reform, economy, abolition of slavery, cheap bread — and that irrespective of party many candidates expressed a greater or less degree of willingness to support those objects in the House of Commons. Brougham and Burdett were probably right in saying that the new parliament would inevitably see great changes; and in that case it was clear that Wellington's minority Government, if it could not direct those changes, was bound to give way to another. But in the elections themselves, even those relatively few contested after 2 August, it is difficult to discern that the news of the French revolution was more than an accidental and superficial feature. Certainly there is little indication that the electors consciously thought of themselves as following in the footsteps of the Paris revolutionaries. The English public was immensely interested in the July revolution, but its attitude resembled less the deference of an admiring disciple than the more characteristic posture of John Bull giving comfortable and mildly patronizing approval to the belated efforts of a less fortunate neighbour. What coloured in retrospect the circumstances in which the general election of 1830 was fought, was the fact that it was followed by a disturbed autumn, the resignation of Wellington's government early in the new session, and its replacement by a new Ministry courageous enough to bring forward a measure of parliamentary reform that is still a landmark in British political history. But that, in the summer of 1830, was hidden in the future; and it was left to another general election to win the battle of reform.

The Catholic Question, Party Fragmentation, and Reform

A. A. ASPINALL

A. A. Aspinall (born 1901) has edited several diaries and the correspondence of Charles Arbuthnot, George III, and George IV. Among his publications are *The Formation of Canning's Ministry, February to August, 1827* (1937), *Lord Brougham and the Whig Party* (1927) and articles on the Canningites. In this selection, Aspinall contends that the movement for parliamentary reform was started within Parliament rather than by external pressure, and by members of the Protestant and landed interests rather than by the middle class.

EIGHTEEN-THIRTY, a year of revolution on the Continent, witnessed in England a change of sovereign and a change of Government, and the beginning of a struggle for parliamentary reform which might well have ended with a revolution in these islands too. . . .

For some time before the change of Government the parliamentary situation had been more than usually obscure. Since the beginning of the century there had been ten Administrations, only one of which had come to an end through forfeiture of the confidence of the House of Commons. Not one of the seven General Elections had failed to give the Government of the day a working majority in the Lower House. . . . Ever since the introduction of the Catholic Relief Bill in 1829 Wellington's had been a minority Government, the first of its kind since Shelburne's, and it survived until November 1830 only because the various groups other than "the party of the Duke's" had failed to combine to defeat it on a question of first-rate importance. At the end of August 1830 Lord Lyndhurst, the Lord Chancellor, claimed that, at the elections, Ministers had gained 23 seats, but according to Opposition calculations they had lost anything between 20 and 50.

This striking difference between the two estimates illustrates the fluidity of the political situation and the looseness of the connections of many members with the party organizations. . . . The voting on 15 November was 233 v. 204; a few other members paired off, and some others made it known how they would have voted had they not been accidentally shut out of the lobby or otherwise prevented. About two-thirds of the members were therefore present, or their views known. The Treasury list of 656 (out of a total membership of 658), is divided under the following heads:

1. *Friends* (311). Ministers themselves admitted, therefore, that "the party of the Duke's" was a minority party. As many as 17 of them voted against the Government, or paired off. Among them was Charles Tyrell, member for Suffolk, who, Planta had told Peel on 13 August, "will certainly be a friend." He had added, "Essex is safe for Colonel Tyrell and Western." The former was one of the seventeen, the latter was subsequently placed by the Treasury itself among the "Foes." A fourth county member, Lord Acheson, admittedly had a "crotchet," and by the name of J. L. Lee, member for Wells, appears the pencilled comment, "not known."

From A. A. Aspinall, *Three Early Nineteenth-Century Diaries* (London, 1952), pp. xiv, xx–xxix. Reprinted by permission of Ernest Benn Ltd.

2. *Moderate Ultras* (37), "nine of which at least I should call friends." Twenty voted against the Government, including three "friends," two "sincere friends" and Lord G. Lennox, who "always votes with us." Sir E. Kerrison "asks for patronage" and presumably got none, as he voted against. By the name of G. Rochfort, an Irish county member, who also voted with the Whigs, there appears the comment, "asks for patronage: don't give it." Serjeant Lefroy, who represented Dublin University, "said he was not opposed to Government. Will oppose." The Treasury was quite right, he did.

3. *Doubtful favourable* (37), "of which I make 18 to be generally friends." He was right about eight of these, including John Phillpotts of Gloucester ("surely he will be a friend"). But five "friends," who were described individually as "a friend where not pledged," voted against the Government. Fourteen out of the 37 supported the Whigs. Of the absentees Mr. Prittie was "a friend with patronage."

4. *Very doubtful* (24), "among whom I reckon three if not four friends." Eleven of them voted against Ministers, but six voted for, including James Loch ("he should be a favourable doubtful at least").

5. *Foes* (188), a solid phalanx of Whigs, plus a few Radicals and country gentlemen Whiggishly inclined. There was no miscalculation here: not one voted contrary to expectation. Nicholson Calvert "will not be uniformly opposed," but on 15 November, at any rate, he voted with the Whigs. To Lord Brabazon was attached the comment, "I hear from Ireland that he is to be *soothed.*"

6. *Violent Ultras* (25), two of whom, surprisingly enough, voted with Ministers on the 15th.

7. *Doubtful unfavourable* (23), "of which I have put a query to four." Only one in this group voted with Ministers.

8. *The Huskisson party* (11), which, apart from the two absentees, voted solidly to turn out the Government.

The 82 English county members represented more "public opinion" than any other group in Parliament, and it is significant that only 15 voted with the Government. Moreover, only two of the 15 were re-elected for their counties at the General Election in the spring of 1831. Forty-nine voted with the Whigs, and two others were accidentally prevented from voting in the same lobby. Of the 16 absentees, eight were on the Treasury list as "friends," seven as "foes" and one as "very doubtful." Had all the county members been present, therefore, not more than 23 would have supported Ministers. The number might well have been smaller, for six county members classified by the Treasury as "friends" voted with the Whigs.

The Whig Abercromby believed that the new Parliament would be the most uncontrollable that had ever met, for the Commons consisted of "the strangest medley that was ever got together in St. Stephen's." Croker, the Secretary of the Admiralty, admitted that the elections had turned out badly for the Government:

Not one man elected in any *contested* place (except, I believe, Bristol) on ministerial principles. Whigs and ultra Tories and Radicals and Reformers and economists were everywhere successful against those who stood on the Government interest. I know that this is not the light in which the Treasury views the Returns, but I see in them the seeds of the most troublesome and unmanageable Parliament since that of 1640 which overturned the monarchy and beheaded the monarch.

Yet the elections need not have been fatal to the Government: had Wellington pursued a different policy, strengthening his Ministry by taking in the Canningites and some of the moderate Whigs, and agreeing to a very modest measure of parliamentary reform, he might have survived. He attributed his defeat to two events: the July Revolution in France, and the concession of Catholic emancipation. Doubtless he exaggerated the importance of the first, for a great many of the election contests were over by the time the news of the revolution in Paris reached England. The country was just emerging from the trough of a trade depression; wages were low, unemployment widespread, and, said the Duke, men fancied that they had only to follow the example of the Parisians in order to recover their prosperity. In many constituencies, therefore, he added, candidates were required to pledge themselves to vote for parliamentary reform and a policy of retrenchment.

Of much greater consequence were the effects of Catholic emancipation, which had fatally split the Tory party. The process of disintegration, indeed, had begun long before the great "betrayal" in 1829. That section of the party which stood, in religion, for the preservation of Anglican supremacy on both sides of St. George's Channel, and in politics for the maintenance of the privileged position of the landed interest, had for some years been increasingly dissatisfied with the fiscal, currency and agricultural policy of successive Tory Administrations. The protection given to agriculture by the corn laws had been substantially reduced in 1828. Mrs. Arbuthnot had noted the distressing effects of the temporary Corn Bill of 1826 on the unity of the party. Lord Liverpool, then Prime Minister, had been obliged to make it a question of confidence:

He succeeded, and had a large majority, but it was chiefly composed of the Opposition, and many of Lord Liverpool's oldest and firmest adherents such as the Dukes of Northumberland and Newcastle, Lord Hertford, Lord St. Germans, &c., either voted against us or stayed away. Our party, as a party, is entirely broke up.

During the last years of the Liverpool Ministry Huskisson and Robinson had scaled down the protection given to manufacturers. With growing consternation Tory country gentlemen watched the progress of this policy embodying the principles of the new political economy which they were confessedly incapable of understanding. Then, in April 1827, came an open rupture when Canning succeeded Lord Liverpool. His foreign policy since 1822 had been opposed by his High Tory colleagues, and more than forty Ministers, including half the Cabinet, resigned rather than serve under him.

It was in the hope of re-uniting his shattered party that Wellington reluctantly accepted the premiership in January 1828. But this hope was not realised, and, indeed, his policy during the next two years completed the party's disintegration. He quarrelled with the liberal Tories led by Huskisson, and their secession at the end of May 1828 deprived the Administration of some of its ablest members. The concession of Catholic emancipation a year later thoroughly alienated from the Government the ultra Tories, whose leader, the Duke of Cumberland, now described Wellington as the most dangerous Minister the country had ever had — for he meant to overthrow the monarchy itself as well as the Protestant Church in Ireland. . . . Two hundred and two ministerialists and others (including tellers and pairs) voted against the Government during the progress of the Relief Bill through the Commons. They included exactly half the English county members, the independent country gentlemen. The outraged ultras believed that the Church of England and the Protestant Constitution as established by the Revolution Settlement were in mortal danger now that Catholics might buy their way into the House of Commons in large numbers *via* the rotten boroughs. But the revolt against Peel's leadership in 1829 was very different from that of 1846. Without a man of genius like Disraeli to lead them, they remained an unorganised faction. Nevertheless, they brought about the downfall of the Wellington Ministry in 1830.

The Government never expected that the ultras would continue their hostility. Most of them, indeed, did not do so. Of the 202 dissidents, 145 were re-elected at the General Election in the summer of 1830 (and one more at a subsequent by-election). Of these 145 only 34 voted against the Wellington Ministry on 15 November, though many of the 57 absentees would probably have done so had they been present. The remaining 54 voted with Ministers.

It was not a united Opposition which defeated the Duke, but a fortuitous combination of half-a-dozen groups hitherto acting separately. "Connexions" within the two-party systems had long existed, but, from a variety of causes, these groups were more than usually numerous in 1830:

1. A small number of Radicals who on most occasions voted against the Government irrespective of its composition.

2. Under the leadership of O'Connell there was already the nucleus of an Irish Radical party, the formation of which had been made possible by the Catholic Relief Act. The repeal of the Union was to be its principal aim, although the question of parliamentary reform soon took priority as the more immediately practicable.

3. The Whigs who, in the spring and early summer, had been re-united under the leadership of Grey and Althorp.

4. The remains of the Canningite party, consisting of about thirteen members of the Commons and approximately the same number of peers, and led, until his tragic death on 15 September 1830, by Huskisson, and subsequently by Palmerston.

5. The ultra Tories, the "King's Friends," as they called themselves, with the Duke of Cumberland as their nominal leader in the Lords, Sir Edward Knatchbull in the Commons. This group was itself divided into two sections, one opposing, the other supporting parliamentary reform.

6. A small Tory group including a few discontented individuals such as Lord Anglesey and his supporters in the Commons, together with the remnants of the Grenville connexion, which had already split into two fragments, the friends of Charles Wynn, and the followers of his foolish and ambitious relative, the Duke of Buckingham and Chandos, who for eight years had been dissatisfied with all Governments because they would not recognise his absurd claims to Cabinet office. With his

seven votes in the Commons he was prepared to join the Ministry — any Ministry — in return for an appropriate offer of place.

Wellington was doubtless right in saying that there was a noticeable absence of principle in this variegated Opposition. "At the present moment," he declared, "there is very little difference of principle among public men in general. The opposition is, generally speaking, *personal.*" "Party," remarked Lord Holland in February 1830, "seems to be no more." "With respect to Whigs and Tories *now,*" said the Duke of Cumberland at the same time, "it appears to me that that idea should be laid completely aside." The Radical Sir Francis Burdett thought so too: he hoped that the out-of-date distinctions between Whigs and Tories had been buried in the grave of the Capulets. Huskisson had said at the beginning of 1829 that the only great party division would be that between Catholic and anti-Catholic. A few weeks later that fateful question was settled. No great party division again emerged until March 1831, and even then, many of the opponents of the Reform Bill supported parliamentary reform in principle.

The absence of serious difference of opinion among public men afforded ample opportunities of strengthening the Wellington Ministry, for, in the summer of 1830 many Opposition members were ready and even anxious to join. Lord Althorp admitted that the Duke had done more for the good of the country than any preceding Prime Minister. Wellington, therefore, owed his defeat in November to his reluctance to share power with the leading members of some of the Opposition groups. The veto on Lord Grey's return to office disappeared with the death of George IV, and the Duke's decision not to make room for him drove Grey into open opposition just at the close of the Session. And the passing of the Catholic Relief Bill had not only opened up possibilities of co-operation between the Wellington Ministry and Opposition groups; it had removed, on the other hand, the great barrier to a union of Whigs and ultra Tories, and the emergence of the question of parliamentary reform was soon to create a party bond between some of them, at any rate.

The Reform Ministry, therefore, was not so much a Whig Ministry as a non-Party Government representing, with the exception of the Radicals, all the groups which had combined to defeat the Duke. It was formed to satisfy the tempestuous demand in the country for an efficient measure of parliamentary reform. Soon after this aim had been triumphantly achieved, the Government, naturally enough, shed practically all its non-Whig elements except the Canningites, who became permanently incorporated in the Whig party. This lack of homogeneity was reflected in the weakness of its parliamentary position. The Whigs themselves were a minority party as they had been before 1830, and their Government depended for its existence on support from the Opposition benches — sometimes Radical, sometimes Tory.

Like the Peelites in the Aberdeen Ministry later, the Canningites had a representation in the Cabinet extravagantly disproportionate to their parliamentary strength: all three Secretaryships of States, and the Presidentship of the Board of Control. Of the regular Tories, Lord Anglesey returned to Ireland as Lord Lieutenant; Charles Wynn became Secretary at War, and Lord Wellesley took one of the great Household offices. Lady Spencer would have liked to see Sir Henry Hardinge, one of Wellington's ministerial colleagues, in the Grey Cabinet, for he lived on the most friendly terms with Spencer House, and his refusal of office, it was thought, was probably grounded more on his attachment to the Duke than on any considerable difference of opinion. And Lord Lyndhurst, the Lord Chancellor in the Wellington Ministry, would certainly have remained in office but for Brougham's contemptuous refusal of the Attorney-Generalship.

The Duke of Richmond, as Postmaster-General, represented the ultra Tories in the Cabinet. Their leader in the Commons, Sir Edward Knatchbull, was also thought of for a Cabinet office, for he too had become a convert to parliamentary reform, though he was to find the Reform Bill too revolutionary to support. Many of his friends were perfectly sincere and consistent in advocating parliamentary reform. When in 1829 the High Church party found its opinions suddenly disregarded on the question which they had always considered to be the most important in the whole range of politics, they naturally began to think that there was something wrong with the composition of a Parliament which could bring about such a disastrous result. Fear that the Irish supporters of O'Connell, and wealthy English Catholics like the Duke of Norfolk might secure a substantial representation in the Commons by way of the rotten boroughs made many Tories parliamentary reformers. The Marquess of Blandford, the son of the Duke of Marlborough, said in June 1829 that this process had already begun. As early as 1822 Thomas Grenville had remarked that some country gentlemen in Parliament were opposing the Government's agricultural policy as affording quite inadequate protection to the agricultural interest. "Some who were steady anti-Reformers have suffered themselves to be gulled by Cobbett into attributing the pressure of their rents to an inadequate representation in Parliament." Lord Blandford said that, but for the rotten boroughs, the Government would have been unable to change the country's fiscal policy, nor would it have had such a large majority in favor of the Catholic Relief Bill which had overthrown the Constitution. Parliament, he maintained, had ceased to represent public opinion. The Protestant Constitution and the security of the landed interest, of trade, and of industry, would remain in danger so long as Government majorities were to be obtained by trafficking in seats. Knatchbull, too, had been alarmed as much for the future of English agriculture as for the security of the Anglican Church. He spoke despondingly about the deplorable effects on agricultural prices of the currency changes since 1819. "If Old England should go on." "If we shall last for five years." Expressions such as these revealed the depths of his despair. Lord Mahon, who had supported the Wellington Ministry, wrote in December 1830:

Nothing ever loosed the bonds of political union on our side, nothing ever split up families or destroyed political friendships so dangerously to the State as the mode in which *that great* question [catholic emancipation] was *settled.* . . . The classes of men among whom Reform has made such important advances are the influential and the staunchest Protestants — the Protestant gentry and the Protestant clergy who, if you get the soundest of them sometimes in private by their firesides will tell you, very many of them, that the House of Commons does not properly represent the people, or *that measure* could not have been SO carried.

Of the 145 ultra Tories re-elected in 1830, six were no longer in Parliament by 22 March 1831 when the division on the Reform Bill took place, but as one other was returned after the division on 15 November 1830, 140 could have voted on 22 March. Of these as many as 106 found the Bill too thorough-going and voted against it; 28 supported it and there were six absentees. Five of the six voted against the Government on 19 April (supporting Gascoyne's wrecking amendment). So 111 ultras voted against the Bill, but many of them would have supported a more moderate measure.

Reform — A Means to an End

THE WESTMINSTER REVIEW

The *Westminster Review* was the mouthpiece of the Radicals. Opposed to the two "props" of the aristocracy, the Church and the Law, the *Westminster Review* took its position on political reform in its first issue in 1824. "What we desire is, to place the right of voting for members of parliament on such a footing, that it shall not be for the interest of the voter to give his suffrage from any other motive than the verdict of his conscience, preferring the fittest man." In this selection, the *Review* argues that the Bill at best was a compromise and that the ministers, pledged to grant reform, had to effect it through legal means under the old constitutional system. This explains the kind of bill the Whigs introduced in Parliament.

THE TRIUMPH of the Reformers may now be considered as achieved. The appeal of the King to the sense of the people, has been answered in a manner that precludes all doubt or misconception. The most sceptical must believe, the most ignorant perceive, that the old constitution of the Commons House of Parliament has now become matter of history. Its glories, its powers, have at length yielded to popular indignation; and at once and for ever have been erased from the category of present existencies.

A step in advance then, has been made by the popular interest; the people have arrived somewhat nearer to the great object of their wishes; a good government is less distant than before. An important question arises, now that the struggle is over. What has our victory attained — what is the step we have made? What degree of benefit may be expected from the measure so triumphantly carried? An answer to this inquiry, with remarks upon some of the proposed regulations which will effect the good, is the object of the following observations: —

In order to render this answer satisfactory, it is requisite to describe shortly, the situation of the country previous to the proposal of reform. The object of the present inquiry is, not to learn in what degree the new constitution approximates to that which we may deem perfection (that, at present, would be an unnecessary as well as ungracious inquiry); but to discover in how much it may be considered an improvement on the former parliament.

Every one must know, that whatever might have been the desires of the present ministry, they could have done no more than they have done. The reform they have proposed is unexpectedly extensive — had they been willing to have rendered it still more sweeping, in their situation prudence would have confined their endeavours to something similar to the measure they have actually brought forward. Let it not be supposed, however, that it is intended to be insinuated that the ministers have themselves any ulterior reforms in view. At present, there is no need of an inquiry into this matter; but we do wish to be understood as most distinctly asserting, that considering the ministerial plan of reform as emanating either from hearty well-wishers to a perfect government, or from prudent ministers acting for the aristocratic party, it is deserving of the most strenuous approval and support. And this apparent paradox is explained by

From *Westminster Review*, XV (July, 1831), pp. 149–52.

the single circumstance, that the opposition of the aristocracy on the one hand would have rendered impossible any complete reform, at least without an attempt at civil war; while, on the other, had not some concession been made, and that a large one, the people would have risen in rebellion; and the miseries of the commotion that would necessarily have followed, would, even in the opinion of the aristocracy, have been an evil more terrible than their present loss of power. The sequel will shew, that we are no very great admirers of the present ministers, or the party to which they belong. We are, therefore, the more desirous of frankly awarding them that large measure of approbation to which they are so justly entitled. This approbation is offered, not because they have spontaneously proposed a measure which is greatly conducive to promote objects we have long strenuously supported; but because they have wisely judged the signs of the time, have prudently gone with the onward march of events, and have abstained from meeting the national advance by any headstrong and blind opposition, which would necessarily have involved this country in dreadful commotion, and inevitably have rooted out themselves and the whole class to which they belong.

Waiving all consideration of right on the part of the people; avoiding all examination of their claims, abstaining from placing the defence of the ministerial plan of reform on the score of the justice of these claims: we are here prepared to maintain, that on the grounds of mere expediency, reform was absolutely necessary. The bill itself is full of anomalies (these will be immediately considered), they have been supported, as well as attacked, by contradictory arguments; yet, with all its imperfections, when considered in relation to the circumstances with which it was brought forward, it is a wise, we may say a beneficent measure.

To any one who has bestowed attention on the political condition of the European world, it must be manifest, that within the last fifty years, a new, a constantly increasing, and now almost a paramount power has become an element to be carefully estimated in all political considerations — this power is the power of the people. It has often happened, in former periods, that the will of the great mass of the population has been, for a time, a matter that could not be neglected. But these manifestations of power, were merely outbreakings of a sudden indignation; the result of some peculiar evil, and expiring almost at its birth. The power which we are now considering, is of a very different description. It results from principles that are steadily advancing, and becoming universally prevalent — it is the offspring of Knowledge, not of Passion. Intelligence is daily spreading among the people, and with that intelligence there come a due feeling of their own importance, and an understanding, not merely of some particular and immediate causes of the evils they suffer, but of the whole framework which has so long been employed to control and oppress them. They will not now rise up in angry rebellion against the tax-gatherer, the overseer of the poor, or the petty officers of justice. They well know that the cause of the evils lies deeper; and they feel, and express little hatred against the mere instruments of mischief. A general, continued, increasing feeling of discontent is in existence, founded on increasing information, a discontent guided, as well as produced by reason. This is the new and formidable power to which the last few years have given birth. It is no hasty emanation, no short-lived existence — gradual, slow, and difficult has been its development; the circumstances which gave it birth, will continue and increase it.

In consequence of this new feeling among the people, nations have been completely severed into two distinct and hostile parties, between whom there is maintained a silent, but ever constant struggle. It is known and felt, but not openly avowed; few being willing fairly to meet the great question, which every day is bringing nearer to a decision. In our own country, the difficulty is greater than in any other; and its consequences, unless consummate prudence direct the conduct of those who possess the power of government for the time being, will be a more appalling spectacle than the world ever witnessed. It is needless, it is mischievous, to shut our eyes to the circumstances by which we are surrounded; by refusing to see, we do not change our situation; nor can he who fairly and honestly describes it, be considered to have promoted the dangers he brings to view. No human influence can now destroy the power which has arisen; none can divert it from that onward course it steadily maintains. It will be (and the prophecy will quickly be fulfilled) the sole existing power in the state — all others will yield to, or be merged into it. The aristocratic rule, though apparently in pristine vigour and splendour, is secretly undermined, and will soon totter to its foundation. A new era is at hand, the people will inevitably be paramount. When it is said that the people will be paramount, it is not intended that a part or section of the whole nation, who may be called the people, will domineer over another part who may not be called by that name. What is meant to be expressed is, that all sections of the people considered politically will be merged into one whole: that no part of that whole, no section endowed with privileges will rule over the remainder; no exclusive political rights, so exclusive as to make a class, will exist. The words, people, nation and governing body, will be synonymous.* All politically privileged classes will be abolished. Those who are now the sole rulers, will then only be a part of the governing body. They will not be made slaves, they will only cease to be lords.

* More correctly, nearly synonymous; people under age, lunatics, idiots and criminals, being excluded from the electoral body.

Reform — A Political and Social Movement

THE QUARTERLY REVIEW

The *Quarterly Review* first appeared in 1809. Throughout the 1820's, it supported Lord Liverpool and after 1830, Robert Peel and the Duke of Wellington. Its Toryism was a more rational conservatism than that espoused by *Blackwood's Edinburgh Magazine*. Its columns carried on a steady ideological war with the *Edinburgh Review*, the *Westminster Review*, and at times *Blackwood's*. In this analysis of the reform movement, the *Quarterly Review* describes the agitation as the work of a coalition of dissidents who saw reform as a means to achieve what the *Review* considered incompatible goals.

O F ALL THE revolutions which the last eventful six months have brought to light, there is none which it would be so difficult to reconcile with the ordinary principles of human action, if one could possibly suppose it real, as that revolution of opinion which, we are assured from all quarters, has taken place among the educated and even the upper classes of society in this country, on the question of parliamentary reform.

It must be allowed, that evils deeply rooted and widely extended, the immediate fruits of the speculations and crisis of 1825, aggravated by that operation affecting the currency, of which this Journal has often treated in detail, had been pressing more or less severely on all the productive classes of the community, agricultural, manufacturing, and commercial; and that this pressure, prolonged through a period of unexampled duration, and gaining rather fresh intensity, as it seemed, instead of the usual mitigation, from time, had begun to impair the sources of the revenue, and, by an unhappy concurrence with two bad harvests in succession, and, in particular districts, with the permanent mal-administration of the poor-laws, was sensibly deteriorating the condition of the labouring population. All this is past question. Nor can it be matter of surprise that so much suffer-

ing should have bred some discontent. Of the many persons whose interests are affected by vicissitudes of this nature, few can be supposed to have acquired much knowledge of their elementary causes; — few indeed have been accustomed to reason on such subjects at all. So that, when once fairly thrown out of the track of their ordinary experience, and bewildered by crosses and disappointments neither foreseen nor understood, the weaker easily learn to regard the whole frame of society round them with a sort of mixed feeling of distrust and despair, and their minds become open to the impression of almost any doctrines, the most absurd and anti-social, and at the same time the most discordant from each other, provided only they flatter their present passions, hold out some vain promise of bettering their condition, or throw the blame of that condition on those whose lot in life has been more fortunate than their own.

Such is very much the course of discipline which, during four cheerless years, had been left to operate almost uncontrolled on the minds of the working classes, the artisans, retail dealers, and many of the smaller capitalists throughout England. Early in the spring of last year, however, a better dawn began to appear. We shall be supported, we believe, by the testimony of the most practised observers, when we

Quarterly Review, XLIV (February, 1831), pp. 555–558; XLV (April, 1831), pp. 252–253, 278–283.

state that, during some succeeding months, the increase of consumption and the rise of prices were simultaneous and progressive — that the workmen throughout the manufacturing districts were already in pretty full employment, the markets for colonial produce slowly reviving, the funds on the advance, and that, with the promise of an abundant crop on the ground, the whole face of industry was resuming that healthful complexion to which it had been long a stranger. That this amendment was neither illusory nor superficial, we have the most conclusive proof in the improvement of the revenue, which has, in fact, continued steady and progressive even to the moment at which we write, in spite of all that has recently happened to interrupt the course of commerce, and disturb the foundations of property and order, both at home and abroad. With returning prosperity, the fever of opinion too was subsiding. Finding a renewed source of hope and interest in their private affairs, men were perplexing themselves less with those of the state. And though, in particular instances, the seeds of disquiet and disaffection might have taken too deep a hold to be so quickly eradicated, and the common traders in sedition had relaxed nothing of their wonted activity, it may safely be affirmed that, at the period of his present Majesty's accession, nothing was less expected, or less probable, than the success of any early attempt to disturb materially the established system of the legislature.

Since then, what a change! If there be any faith in the organs of public opinion — if we are to judge from the language of popular meetings — from the all but unanimous voice of the press — from the declarations in parliament itself — before a few short weeks shall have passed over our heads, that parliament of England, so long a prodigy and an enigma in the eyes of surrounding nations — that parliament under whose auspices we have attained our present station in arts and arms, and have contrived for nearly a century and a half to unite the advantages of the most unbounded freedom of discussion, with the most thorough subordination and security of property, — that parliament is to perform a voluntary act of abdication, to declare its own incompetency to exercise its functions any longer with benefit to the nation, and to resign those functions into the hands of a new and unknown body, constituted on other principles!

This "great measure of relief and redress" as it has been called, is demanded, we are told, by the whole country, with an impatience that admits neither of delay nor of compromise. Its advocates (and they have the argument just now very much to themselves) never speak of it but as of a thing quite decided and inevitable. Indeed, they give us very plainly to understand, that we are to have no alternative between that and a bloody revolution. The very idea of its rejection, they treat as a supposition "too monstrous to be thought of for a moment." It is a sort of fulfillment of destiny, in short, about whose possible consequences we need give ourselves no concern, since, do what we may, we can have no hope of escaping it. The newspapers, always echoing the voice which for the time is loudest, throw in their too powerful influence, to work on the enthusiasm of some, and the fears of others. The only question admitted at all, is with respect to the degree and manner of the reform. A person who at any of the later county meetings should have presumed to doubt the soundness of the general principle, would have been hooted down as an idiot. Scarcely even a stray pamphlet ventures to raise its feeble cry on the side of prudence and reflection. And the most illustrious man of our period becomes for a time almost a mark for popular odium, merely because he has the manliness to stand forward alone, and declare his opposition to parliamentary reform, in terms precisely to the same effect as those employed only three years before on a similar occasion by Mr. Canning, at the zenith of his popularity, and amidst the cheers of an applauding, we might almost say of a worshipping, audience.

But the most amusing circumstance of all, (if anything can be deemed amusing where the whole is in truth so melancholy,) is the simplicity with which individuals, the most diametrically opposed to each other in principle,—men who have never before been able to agree on any given proposition—knots of exclusive theorists in politics and political economy, possessed with dogmas the most incompatible, and advocating every one some sovereign specific of his own for the evils which he thinks beset the nation, have yet all submitted themselves to the common prestige, and join, or affect to join, in hailing a consummation, which, as each little antagonist unit fondly imagines, is to bring the little antagonist nostrum of each into active operation. One calls for reform, because it is to be the precursor of unbounded freedom of trade; another sees in it the triumphant revival of the old system of protecting duties and monopoly;—the bullionist relies on a reformed parliament for the defeat of all future attempts to tamper with the metallic currency; while the champion of paper trusts that it may yet save the nation by a copious issue of one-pound notes;—the people of Liverpool hail in its advent the total and instant emancipation of the West Indian slaves:—to the Whig, it is a millennium of office; to Joseph Hume, pounds, shillings and pence; and to the Orangemen of the Standard a repeal of the Catholic Relief Bill:—one set of writers anticipate from reform an immediate extension to Ireland—a measure in their opinion otherwise hopeless—of the English system of poor-rates; while those of an opposite persuasion expect the abrogation of all poor-rates whatsoever:—by reform the annuitant hopes to obtain a repeal of the corn-laws; the landholder a reduction of taxes and the eventual demolition of funded property; the farmer an exemption from tithes AND rent: and the Lancashire operative a rise of wages:—the rioter and the rick-burner trusts through the same powerful engine, to drink wine every day and to swing in a coach;—the dogmatic coxcombs of the school of Bentham, the Spenceans, Owenites, and republicans of all denominations, look to reform for the realization of their Utopian dreams;—and Mr. Daniel O'Connell, not the least sagacious of the array, sees in it a boundless field for never-ending agitation, and is already menacing those, who "at present trample down him and his followers, with punishment and degradation from the strong power of *a reformed parliament.*"

* * *

The Movement is still on the advance, and just now at full tilt. His Majesty's ministers have fairly thrown aside the reins, and, surrendering themselves and the country to its impulse, have adventured on a leap which has astonished equally their friends and their opponents. . . . We return to this momentous question of Parliamentary Reform, under circumstances most materially altered since the date of our last publication. . . . Now, the project of government has, for upwards of six weeks, been before the public: the subject has been canvassed in all its bearings, both in Parliament and out of Parliament, in speech and in print; it has been the unceasing theme of the daily press, and the hourly topic of private conversation; and it may be doubted, if any political question within the memory of man (the Catholic question not excepted) has never engaged, within so short a space of time, so large a share of thought and consideration. . . .

Meanwhile, we may be allowed, perhaps, to detain our readers for an instant while we say a few more words as to the circumstances and origin of this agitation, and in support of the opinion we have from the first professed, that it is an agitation by no means of that formidable character, nor springing from those deep sources which many are prone to believe, but is of a nature quite as evanescent as any other of those periodical excitements to which the people of this country have long been so proverbially subject, and would probably ere this have passed away like its predecessors, but for the factitious influence which it has acquired, from the extraordinary line of conduct which his Majesty's government has thought fit to adopt. And here we meet, in the first place, with that most important and, to this day, uncontroverted fact, which was first brought to the notice of the House of Commons by Mr. Croker, that during the space of six years, from 1824 to 1829, there was not a single petition on the subject of parliamentary reform presented to parliament. . . .

Well, — such was the state of things up to 1829, — when the measure of Catholic emancipation came to agitate and divide the country, and almost entirely to break up the already frittered and discordant Tory party in parliament. At the same time, distresses, which had been gradually encroaching more and more on the springs of industry since 1825, began to press on the lower class with an intensity that was very alarming. Advantage was taken of these circumstances to revive the cry for parliamentary reform; and the note was first sounded from a quarter whence it was least of all apprehended, — from a small band of the High Tories, whom the measures of government had so deeply offended, that for a time every other consideration appeared to be lost in their eagerness to annoy and overturn it. Meanwhile, the Birmingham Political Union was formed: — difficult questions relating to the currency, to free trade, the poor-laws, and other points more or less bearing on the case of the lower orders, began to be declaimed on in a new spirit of wrath and fierceness; advantage was taken of the reluctance, perhaps somewhat indiscreetly manifested by ministers to submit the distresses of the country to parliamentary investigation, in order to hold up such men as the Duke of Wellington and Sir Robert Peel as cold, hard-hearted, unfeeling theorists, individually callous and indifferent to those distresses; the radicals came forth from their lurking places; and, though London continued tolerably quiet, the manufacturing districts began to ring once again with the peals of sedition. — The course pursued by parliament in the case of East Retford is supposed by many to have added to these previously existing elements of combustion; and no doubt it afforded another inflammatory topic, at least in those towns which had expected to profit by the disfranchisement of that borough. But we question if the excitement extended much further. As far as we could observe, the country generally cared very little about the matter. There was no demonstration, at least, in the shape of meetings or petitions, to justify a contrary inference. And we must utterly dissent, at all events, from the now prevailing notion, that a different course of proceeding, on the part of the legislature in that instance, or that any other measure which the legislature could, with the least propriety, have adopted, would have prevented or materially restrained the disorders which, by sympathy with the revolutions of Paris and Brussels, at a subsequent period shook the frame of the commonwealth. Those revolutions unhappily took place at a time when this country was agitated by the struggles of a general election at the commencement of a new reign. Some improvement had indeed by this time begun to show itself in the condition of the population; the spirit of discontent was subsiding; — had time been allowed for the more full development of those seeds of prosperity which were inherent in the system, and have since been sending up their shoots, some excuse might perhaps even have been found for the previous disinclination evinced by ministers to give a too ready ear to the various remedial measures that had been pressed on them; — and that there was no very determined design, on the part of the Ultra-Tories, against the institutions of the state, whatever might have been their personal feelings towards ministers, has since been proved by the fact, that, with one or two exceptions, they were the first to rally round them on the appearance of real danger. Parties, however, were still disunited, — the administration weak, — and all society still smarting from its recent sores, — when these appalling events came like a thunder-cloud to overcast the rising serenity. Faction was not idle to avail herself of the new capacity for mischief, with which circumstances so unexpected and opportune had all at once endowed her. No topic of excitation was spared, which could be likely to inflame the people, or fill them with the idea, that they are the plundered and degraded slaves of a vile oligarchy; and on every hustings the examples of France and Belgium were held up, almost without reserve, as fit objects for imitation. The numbers and the ubiquity of the radical candidates were beyond all precedent. Among other phenomena, the appearance in Yorkshire of Mr. Brougham, in the (to him) novel character of a parliamentary reformer, was not the least portentous. In addressing a meeting of that county in the beginning of August, after reminding them of "that might, slumbering in the arms of temperate freemen, which, though he hoped the fatal experiment never would be tried, he had a confident persuasion would, if it ever should become necessary, be uplifted as manfully as it was by their forefathers, when they marshalled the way, through blood and danger, to a free constitution.". . .

Again, at the Leeds dinner on the 28th September, we find the same eminent individual signalizing his new-born zeal, by the promulgation of a sort of scheme of reform, — a scheme most cautious and innocent indeed, compared to that which he has since sanctioned, though six months ago it was thought sufficiently menacing, — and by declaring that "he would leave in no other man's hands the cause of parliamentary reform. He had assisted others hitherto, but he should now stand forward as the champion of that cause!" — Mr. Hume's speeches, delivered about the same time during the course of a political tour in Scotland, are in a similar vein, or even more inflammatory. As a dinner given to him at Glasgow, he observes, that —

Enough had taken place of late to make men think who had never thought before. The idea

was no longer to be entertained, that treason could be committed only against the King. They had seen a King commit treason against his people; and he hoped they would reflect on what had taken place in France, and they would see, that such a system as that of Scotland never could continue. There were as many now present as would carry a Council by storm!!

The revolutionary flames thus kindled and thus "fanned," spread, as was to be expected, in all directions. A pledge to support parliamentary reform was demanded from many of the other candidates, on the different hustings throughout the country; and, in consequence of its being declined by some of the old members, an unusual proportion of Whigs and radicals, many of them new to parliament, were returned. A powerful attack was now opened on the Wellington administration, through the medium of the press, and particularly by a pamphlet — the second of a series attributed, at the time, to the new member for Yorkshire — which contains the following remarkable passage, in allusion to the then recent events in France: —

The lessons, which the Duke of Wellington may learn from this great event, are neither few nor of light account. First of all, it may teach him that an army is more to be depended on in the field than in the city. Beyond all doubt, he counted on the French troops standing by Charles X and his insensate ministers, and was somewhat staggered when he saw some battalions of those brave men refuse to fire upon their fellow-citizens. Beyond all doubt, also, he expected regular troops, when they did fight, to gain an easy victory over an unarmed rabble. The finest soldiers of Europe beaten by a mob, — the boys of the Polytechnic School destroying five hundred of one regiment, and all the officers but three, — streets in half an hour barricaded, and every house become a garrison, from which the very women and children fired shot, and poured down huge paving stones upon veteran troops! This is the very irregular, unscientific, unmilitary spectacle, which the recent history of France presents to the tacticians of the Horse Guards, and records, for the encouragement of all freemen and the terror of all military tyrants, in all countries and in all times. It is also a page of history which will be read with advantage by the soldiers themselves, of all ranks; and may have some influence on their minds when they are poring over that other page, wherein is recorded the great virtue of those patriotic troops who, in the soldier, forgot not the citizen, and refused to obey the unlawful command that would have pointed their arms to shed the blood of their unoffending countrymen!

This certainly was not to be misunderstood. Meanwhile, the burnings and machine-breakings began to spread in Kent, — a clamour was got up in London between the pickpockets and the newspapers against the new police, — and a most alarming agitation was set on foot in Ireland for the repeal of the union between the two countries. A general consternation spread abroad; many of the upper and educated classes seemed to be quite bewildered and confounded, by the menacing apparitions that were starting up on all sides; and not a few had the weakness to imagine, that by truckling to compulsion, and chiming in with the prevailing frenzy, that they might purchase security. Even the kindliness of heart and popular habits of our excellent sovereign, by giving encouragement to extravagant hopes, rather served to increase the ferment. And, by a piece of hypocritical finesse, which has rarely been neglected through all these agitations, and which remarkably distinguishes them from those which took place at the time of the former French revolution, the most avowed and atrocious purposes of treason were associated, in the same mouth, with the most fulsome professions of loyalty, and the grossest adulation of his Majesty's character and station. — Under these circumstances parliament met. The cry for parliamentary reform, which had been sounded through the country, found an echo within the walls of the house itself. The administration soon discovered, that they had not sufficient strength to carry on the affairs of the government, and were compelled to withdraw and make room for the Whigs, — who entered office under that solemn pledge of "retrenchment, non-intervention, and parliamentary reform," so ill-judged in its origin, and so fatal in its results for their own reputation as statesmen, and for the peace, — it may be, for the ultimate destiny, of their country.

Reform and the Social Structure of
Three English Cities

ASA BRIGGS

Asa Briggs (born 1921), Professor of History and Dean of the School of
Social Studies at the University of Sussex, England, is the author of several
highly readable books which include the *History of Birmingham* (1952), *Victorian
People* (1955), *The Age of Improvement* (1957) and *Chartist Studies* (1959).
In this article, reform becomes a means to different ends as Briggs relates the
politics of reform to the economic and social structure of three provincial cities.

MANY OF THE most important political-cal changes of the nineteenth century have been studied exclusively from the standpoint of London. Clear-sighted contemporaries have been long aware of the consequent misrepresentation. "Londoners are the lapidaries of the nation," wrote Holyoake, "they polish the diamond found in the counties and sometimes if no one challenges them, they take credit for the jewel." Only too often no one has challenged them. The result has not been so much a failure to render credit where credit is due as a failure to understand the mainsprings of national political action. It is only when the local element has obtruded unmistakably, as in the story of Chartism, that it has been examined with care. Where it has not obtruded, historians have often been more willing to accept things as they seemed from the standpoint of the capital rather than to investigate them as they arose.

The purpose of this article is to investigate some of the local features of the reform agitation of 1830–2, particularly in three large unrepresented cities, Birmingham, Manchester and Leeds. 1830 saw the convergence of different local reform movements, each coloured by the social structure and political experience of its area. Be-tween 1831 and 1832 the whig Reform Bill was considered locally to be not so much an end as a means to an end; and the objects which it was intended to secure varied in different parts of the country. "It must be recollected that a Reform in Parliament is only a MEANS to an end," wrote a Newcastle radical, "it is a means offered to the people for electing a more free, bold and honest House of Commons. . . . The ENDS which that House of Commons is to accomplish are yet to be obtained.". . .

In each of the three cities the most important political problem which emerged was that of reconciling two approaches to reform — the approach of popular radicals, stirred by distress and seeking reform as a cure, and the approach of mercantile manufacturing groups, demanding the representation of local interests. Reconciliation was relatively easy in Birmingham where social structure and political leadership encouraged co-operation between all reformers; it was more difficult in Manchester and Leeds, where group interests clashed. After the Reform Bill had been secured, Attwood and Scholefield were returned unopposed in triumph as members for Birmingham, while there were bitter election contests in both Manchester and Leeds. The result was

From Asa Briggs, "The Background of the Parliamentary Reform Movement in Three English Cities
(1830–2)," *Cambridge Historical Review*, IX (1948), pp. 293–295, 297–306, 308–317. Reprinted
by permission of the author and Cambridge University Press.

that Birmingham secured a position of primacy in the reform movement, which persisted until the split inside the Political Union in 1838.

The popular radical approach to reform was well articulated by 1830. It was compounded of three elements — a protest against "distress," a theory of rights, and a dream, or rather a series of often inconsistent dreams, of "a different system after the Reform Bill is disposed of." The theory of rights, inherited from eighteenth-century radicalism, provided a set of slogans and offered a comprehensive political terminology, but behind the theory was the unescapable question asked by Cobbett in 1833: "What did we want the Reform Bill FOR? It certainly was that it might do us some good; that it might better our situation. . . . This was what *the people* wanted the Reform Bill for, and not for the gratification of any abstract or metaphysical whim."

When "distress" reawakened the popular radicals in 1829 and in 1830, they already had their own traditions upon which to rely. In Manchester, Leeds and Birmingham, there were vivid memories of the postwar agitations, particularly of 1819. In Manchester the memory of Peterloo, "the field of blood," was kept alive at annual celebrations. In Leeds, at the radical demonstrations of 1830, the old 1819 banners were carried. In Birmingham, George Edmonds, the Secretary of the Political Union, provided a link between old reformers and new ones. Continuity was never broken. It could have been said of meetings in all three cities in 1830, as it was said of Birmingham, that "we observed some of our veteran reformers of the ancient days come forth, forgetting their years and their infirmities."

The approach of mercantile and manufacturing groups to reform was substantially different. In the debates on Grampound, "the beginning of the end of the old representative system," Lord John Russell underlined the two main reasons for the demand for distinctive local representation — first, the increase in the number of questions relating to trade, the poor laws, taxation, combinations and other social and economic problems, coming before the House of Commons, and secondly, the difference between the station and habits of the county members and their urban constituents. "However well informed they [the county members] may be to do their duty to their constituents . . . they have not the knowledge requisite to study the grievances and wants of manufacturers.". . .

In 1827 and 1828 differences between reformers in Manchester were so wide that they were noted in the House of Commons as a serious obstacle to the transfer of the Penryn seat. The failure of the attempts to secure piecemeal reform emphasized the necessity for more vigorous political action in the localities, whether the old system were to be modified or overthrown. The problem of securing good working relations between all types of reformers was forced to the forefront. "There were materials of discontent enough," Attwood told the first general audience of the Birmingham Political Union in May 1830; "the only difficulty was in making them harmonize and unite in some common remedy." This article sets out to examine more closely social relationships and political leadership in Birmingham, Manchester and Leeds, and their effect upon the politics of reform. In each city the central problem was the same, but in each city there were significant and sometimes wide differences in the approach to it.

There were four features of the social structure of Birmingham which made it possible for Attwood to "harmonize and unite in some common remedy" the diverse elements in local reform circles. The first was the predominance of the small workshop (rather than the factory), where small masters (rather than industrial capitalists) worked in close contact with their skilled artisans. Economic development in Birmingham in the first half of the nineteenth century multiplied the number of producing units rather than added to the scale of existing enterprises. The second was the lack of labour-saving machinery to throw workers out of their jobs.

The operation of mechanism in this town, is to effect that alone, which requires *more force* than the *arm* and the tools of the workman could yield, still leaving his skill and experience of head, hand and eye in full exercise; — so that Birmingham has suffered infinitely less from the introduction of machinery than those towns where it is, in a great degree, an actual *substitute* for human labour. [W Hawkes Smith, *Birmingham and Its Vicinity as a Manufacturing and Commercial District* (1836).]

The third was the marked social mobility, which blurred sharp class distinctions. Small masters might fail in their enterprises and become journeymen again. "On voit bien vite," commented Faucher, "que la bourgeoisie, qui fait partout la base des populations urbaines, ne s'élève guère à Birmingham au-dessus des régimes inférieures de la société." The fourth was the tendency to regular economic fluctuations, during the worst years of which the discontents of both middle classes and working classes, "the bees of society," moved together. Distress did not divide masters and men in Birmingham; it brought them together by producing a common statement of grievances.

The propaganda of Thomas Attwood and the Political Union "of the Lower and Middle Classes of the People," founded in December 1829, emphasized the necessity for class co-operation. Class co-operation indeed was the basis of the Union, currency reform the economic philosophy and the ultimate object of action, and parliamentary reform the means. These three elements were considered indivisible. Without class co-operation, effective organization could not be built up; without parliamentary reform, currency reform could not be accomplished; without currency reform, class conflicts would become serious even in Birmingham, and revolution might eventually break out. Revolution was the final nightmare. If great misery had been created by the breaking up of the French social system during the Revolution, "not a tenth part so complicated as our own social system, what would be the dreadful misery every man would sustain, be he rich or be he poor, if ever the complicated and wonderful machinery of English society were suffered to break up?" [*Report of the Proceedings of the Birmingham Political Union,* 17 May 1830.]

If, in the last resort, Attwood's political philosophy was conservative, his choice of means was essentially opportunist. He began by supporting the tory Marquis of Blandford's reform proposals, born in the atmosphere of protestant bitterness engendered by the passing of Catholic Emancipation. He ended his active career by accepting the Six Points of the Charter. At no stage of his life did he accept the principles of Whiggery, but he was prepared to work with whigs and Benthamite radicals between 1830 and 1832, recognizing as did Joseph Parkes, who disagreed with him profoundly about the currency, "that the present is the most eventful political crisis in the history of the country" and that all local feelings of difference of opinion had to be laid on one side. Between 1830 and 1832, Attwood never identified himself with the powerful anti-whig under-current inside the Union. Edmonds talked of "patriotic teatable politicians, who would never do anything except behind closed doors" and contrasted "the manly conduct of the tories with the insincere dirty conduct of the whigs." Muntz dismissed whigs as "always professing to support the interests of the people, but always acting in opposition to their professions." Attwood, however, always tried hard to maintain the maximum amount of local unity and good will. Of Grey, for instance, he later said, "I looked at his unsullied character with something approaching to reverence."

The Birmingham Political Union provided a model organization, while the struggle for the Reform Bill went on. . . . It was the Political Union which rallied the men of 1819, collected grievances, marshalled arguments and organized crowds. The *Times* called it "the barometer of the Reform feeling throughout England," and as the impulsive Dr. Wade did not fail to point out, it was capable in emergency of becoming a national thermometer too, "rising to *fever heat* with rage, indignation and vengeance."

Attwood's skilled political leadership restrained the over-exuberance of some of his followers. In public he emphasized the lawful character of his organization; in private, admissing some of its weaknesses, he was proud that he had created a popular instrument to secure well thought-out demands. For him the Political Union was a popular agency, which might secure what he had failed to secure by personal appeals to ministers and men of affairs — currency reform. Attwood's economic theories were unorthodox, but they were consistent, and they coloured the whole reform movement in Birmingham. Far from being the wild outpourings of a single-minded crank, they had great political importance. They provided a theory to fit the facts of unemployment and distress in Birmingham, and a basis for common action within the local social framework. Whatever abstract difficulties they presented, they were sufficiently interesting to attract an audience of 1300 at the debate on currency questions between Cobbett and Attwood in1832. Attwood's currency theories grew out of his experiences as a country banker and his alarm at local fluctuations in output and prices. They were a product of Birmingham, but they allowed for a development of mutual understanding with other groups outside — rural country bankers, disgruntled agriculturalists, ultra-tories. While the *Manchester Guardian* was beginning to depict the landlord as the villain of society, the Birmingham currency school, advocating high prices and abundant credit, could find strange allies outside. "You must not think I have no respectable men on my side in politics," Attwood wrote to his tory wife in the middle of the reform struggle; "all landowners are with me, although few of them have the courage to own it."

The question of the corn laws was not completely ignored in Birmingham in 1830–2, but it was subordinated to the currency question. In July 1831, Muntz, presiding over the second annual meeting of the Political Union, claimed that there were two possible ways to prosperity after reform itself had been secured — repeal of the corn laws or reform of the money laws. He threw all his energies into the latter campaign, he said, for to repeal "the corn laws *without altering the money laws* would be certain ruin to the landed interest, because they had *upon the average* mortgaged their estates for half their present value." Attwood hoped that a solution to economic difficulties would be arrived at, where no one would suffer, not even the landed interest, but "it was the duty of the landed interest to devise the means of supporting the high wages of labour, if they retain a law to support the high value of their produce." Although he came to support repeal of the corn laws, he never indulged in vituperation against the landed interest as such, and was prepared at times to express himself more strongly against the industrial middle classes and more particularly against "the monied interest of the City of London."

In time Attwood's currency views ceased to appeal to the industrial classes of Birmingham, and the corn law repeal formula, imported from Manchester, captured the city just at the same time that it became the central point of orthodox applied economics in the country as a whole, but between 1830 and 1832 Attwood's ideas were dominant, and his organization supreme. The Political Union, at first "thought by political men of all parties to be a mere ebullition, which would speedily pass away," had been forged into a powerful instrument at exactly the right time. "We have reason to know," wrote the *Political Union Register,* "that Mr. Attwood had long had the project in contemplation, and we must admit that the prudence with which he has ever directed the Union, was guaranteed to us by that sagacity which enabled him to select the exact time for the formation of that Union."

While the Union rallied reformers in all parts of the country and Attwood became in Place's opinion "the most influential man in England," the way was prepared locally for the great election triumph of Attwood and Scholefield in December 1832. They were both returned unopposed, and toured the streets of the city in an open car drawn by six grey horses amid the cheers of the entire population. The demonstration was a proof of substantial local unity, which would have been impossible in either Manchester or Leeds. The election programme was broad enough to appeal to all — "to stay the march of Anarchy — to relieve the general Distress — to rectify the general wrongs — to secure a full measure of Justice, Liberty and Prosperity to all, and to unite all classes and all sects of my countrymen in peace, happiness and contentment."

If Birmingham was a city of united opinion and co-operative effort, Manchester was a city of cleavages, of social separation and often of open class antagonism. Its most important economic unit was the factory, for although there were large numbers of non-factory workers, the factory workers were more important than in any other city. The factories themselves were often large — in 1832, average employment in the Manchester spinning mills was over 400, and two large firms employed more than a thousand people. The Manchester factory owner, who had made his way forward by thrift and hard work, was already separated by a wide gulf from his workers. In times of bad trade, as in 1829, there was open hostility between spinners and masters. It was in that year that the combination of workers "assumed a formidable and systematic shape" when John Doherty, who had migrated to Lancashire in 1815, built up the National Union of Operative Spinners to fight drastic wage reductions. Doherty, like other spinners before him, although conscious of "the misrepresentation of the people," was sceptical of reform unless it involved social readjustment, based on the right of workmen to "the whole produce of their labour." "Universal suffrage means

nothing more than a power given to every man to protect his own labour from being devoured by others."

The Manchester spinners were the aristocracy of local labour; alongside them the handloom weavers faced the daily challenge of the machine, their condition growing worse as the factory system developed. They were always a threat to local good order even when they were not actively engaged in machine-breaking or in political demonstrations. Francis Place noted how there were large sections of working-class opinion in Manchester, concentrated among the handloom weavers, which hoped for revolution rather than reform, "a revolution in which they might gain, but could not lose."

If the extremism of considerable numbers of the working classes in Manchester was the first reason why it was impossible for a middle-class leader in the city to manage the reform agitation in the same way that Attwood managed the agitation in Birmingham, the second reason was the caution of large numbers of the middle classes themselves in their approach to reform. There was little middle-class interest in large-scale parliamentary reform in Manchester before 1830 except in clearly defined radical circles. As late as June of that year, the *Manchester Guardian* was praising the Wellington régime for doing more "in the way of adapting our institutions to the change and exigencies of the times, than any which has preceded it, or any which would be likely to be formed in its stead." Although the Revolution in France quickened interest in reform in Manchester and the formation of the Grey government was applauded locally, there were few demonstrations of enthusiasm among influential manufacturing and merchant groups.

The exception was the small but "determined band" of middle-class radicals led by Archibald Prentice, who were shocked by the abuses of the "old system," particularly by the continued existence of the corn laws, and who tried to secure united action in Manchester on the basis of "cheap bread" and "thorough reform." Prentice, like Attwood, believed that middle-class and working-class discontents and grievances moved together. He wrote in 1829:

The want of a thorough reform in the Commons House of Parliament will be treated as the great source of the poverty, misery and crime that reigns among the labouring classes of the country; of the dreadful prevalence of embarrassment and insolvency among the middle classes, and the shameless, abandoned political profligacy, which has scattered to the winds of heaven the hereditary respect of Englishmen for the aristocracy of their native land.

Unlike Attwood, Prentice found it difficult both to win the support of the middle classes and to secure the confidence of the working classes. Indeed, it was his most bitter complaint that "the two classes were ranged against each other in a hostility which daily grew more bitter, each taking that antagonistic position to the other that they should have taken against what occasioned the distress of both — ruinous restrictions on trade and a heavy aggravation of the burthen of taxation . . . without a corresponding reduction of the public expenditure."

There was no effective theory in Manchester to bring the classes nearer together in the same way that Attwood's currency panaceas did in Birmingham. Sometimes, indeed, the retrenchment and *laissez-faire* economic doctrines of local cotton manufacturers widened rather than narrowed the gap between the classes, and even the repeal of the corn laws or their modification, which was conceived of by the manufacturers as one of the first fruits of parliamentary reform in the same way that currency reform was in Birmingham, seemed to offer only dubious benefits to factory workers. In 1830–2 the Manchester merchants and manufacturers had not yet discovered their Cobdens and Brights to shape for them a programme, which, even though limited in its appeal, would talk of social justice as well as economic expediency. . . .

Prentice's statement of the case for the repeal of the corn laws aimed at securing widespread working-class support. Although it did not secure it, it is clear that the emphasis on corn in the reform politics of Manchester can be related to local social and economic conditions just as clearly as the emphasis on currency in Birmingham. While the small Birmingham manufacturers looked to high wages, high profits and high prices as indices of economic prosperity, the Manchester manufacturers put their trust in low wages, competitive profits and cheap prices. While the iron interests of the midlands were insular in outlook, preoccupied with an expansionist credit policy at home, the Manchester cotton lords were internationalist in outlook, surveying, with eager interest, movements in international prices and on the exchanges. "Their attention is drawn as naturally to questions of Custom and Excise, as that of the farm labourer to the state of the weather in the time of harvest." In 1830 Manchester cotton accounted for more than half the export trade in manufactured goods, and the attitude of the mill-owner was summed up by J. Deacon Hume in 1833, as "I must have the world for my workshop, and the world for my customer." Against such a local background, opposition to the corn laws became natural and inevitable, and the landlord began to appear as the real villain of society. The basic ideas of the Manchester School were as surely rooted in local soil as were the basic ideas of Attwood and the Birmingham economists. As Dicey pointed out, "Manchester's political theory was shaped by the practical inferences that it drew from commercial experience.". . .

The open divergences between different local groups were reflected in December 1832 at the first election in Manchester, which was a bitterly fought contest between five candidates — Philips, a local liberal cotton merchant; Loyd, a whig banker; Poulett Thomson, a radical free trader and Benthamite, supported by the Prentice group; Hope, a tory churchman; and Cobbett, the popular radical. Out of this jumble of names, the middle-class *Manchester*

Guardian merely wanted a member with an intimate knowledge of the cotton trade, who would understand "the interests of this great community," and save the city of trouble and expense of deputations "dancing in anxious attendance upon the ministers and public boards." Cobbett claimed that such narrow vision was only justified if Parliament was merely a Chamber of Commerce, and advocated instead his own social programme, which would prevent the Reform Bill from becoming a "barren measure" and which would ensure future prosperity, "better victuals and better clothes."

The two most important features of the election were a tory-radical alliance between the defeated candidates Cobbett and Hope and the emergence of the nucleus of the later Anti-Corn Law League around the sponsors of the successful candidates, Poulett Thomson and Philips.

The tory-radical alliance, prophesied by the *Manchester Guardian* before the poll, was not strong enough to emerge victorious, but it was strong enough to reveal a widespread local suspicion of whiggery, which was considered as a common enemy. Cobbetter received most plumpers[1] — 283 — and he shared 302 votes with Hope. Manchester toryism had not been strong enough before the election to mobilize radical antagonism against the whigs as it did in Leeds, but the "unholy alliance of tory and radical" was strong enough to continue sporadically in the 1830's, particularly at the time when incorporation and the police question were interesting the public.

It was less effective locally, however, than the holy alliance of nonconformists, shop-keepers, and radical merchants and manufacturers, which went on to organize the Anti-Corn Law League. Yet even the holy alliance was sceptical of traditional whig principles. At the celebration dinner in December 1832 Philips spoke of the sunset of "pure whiggery," and Poulett Thomson looked forward to a "temperate but searching reform of all our institutions." These advancing horizons pointed to the new politics of the late thirties and forties, but they did not offer much hope to those left in 1832 outside "the pale of the constitution." While Attwood moved ahead in Birmingham from the Reform Bill to the Charter, the Manchester members made no new points of contact with the unrepresented. To Faucher and Engels, writing in the 1840's, Manchester was more than ever a city of suspicion and antagonism.

Leeds differed from Manchester in the relative newness of its most important social and economic changes, which had taken place since the turn of the century. In 1796 there had only been six or seven steam engines working for mills in Leeds, and one for a dyeing house. In 1830 there were 225. The expansion of machinery and the growth of the factory system had revolutionary effects on local social structure. . . .

Rapid changes in the social structure of Leeds and its district produced a first generation of discontented and displaced men, some of them former master clothiers, who were forced into employment in subordinate positions in the mills, which had helped to supersede them. What was true of the Leeds cloth industry was even more conspicuously true of worsted production, which was centred on Bradford, and which by 1830 was a large-scale factory industry. Indeed, the whole district west of Leeds was an area of contrast and conflict. . . .

Between 1830 and 1832 the industrial struggle in Leeds centred round the introduction of machinery, and relations between employers and workers dominated all other issues. The result was that while the mill-owners and merchants were pressing forward for a plan of political reform, based

[1] In a multi-member constituency until 1867 each voter could cast as many votes as there were seats to be filled at the election. But he was not required to cast all the votes he could cast. A plumper is a man who votes only for one candidate in an election, even though he may have two votes. Clearly, for a candidate, this is the most desirable type of voter, because it means that his other vote will not enhance the numbers of another candidate who might keep the first candidate out. In this election, the plumpers whom Cobbett received voted only for him. The others gave one vote to Cobbett and another to Hope.

on support for the whig government and the rights of the £10 householder, the working classes were being stirred not for parliamentary reform, but for factory reform. Two distinct and competing agitations emerged, each with its own separate chronology.

The character of the two agitations was reflected in the outlook and personalities of the two main antagonists — Edward Baines, who had become editor of the vigorous whig *Leeds Mercury* in 1801, and Michael Sadler, tory M.P. — for a rotten borough — and religious philanthropist. Baines believed in the principles of pure whiggery, in so far as they could remain pure in a smoky atmosphere. His approach to the Reform Bill was based on considerations of principle. His son wrote how in 1832 Baines had centred his attention on "the crying abuses of the old system — the represented boroughs without inhabitants, the unrepresented boroughs with a population and wealth like those of capital cities, the extreme and ridiculous inequalities in the extent of the suffrage, the enormous expense and great temptations to corruption and debauchery attendant upon elections of seven or fifteen days' continuance, the inconvenience of having only one polling place for large counties, the heavy cost of out-voters, and other evils which the Reform Bill remedied." He regarded the passing of the Reform Bill "as one of those peaceful constitutional victories, which are the glory of England — victories the fruit of extending knowledge . . . which speak a national sense of justice . . . and which contrast so happily with revolutions of violence and blood." Approaching the Reform question in these terms it is not surprising that he was active in persuading the Yorkshire whig electors to choose Brougham as a candidate in 1830, and the Leeds whig electors to choose Thomas Macaulay in 1832.

Sadler was an old tory irritated by the advance of industry. From 1829 onwards he went out of his way to stress the positive reforms which he believed would help factory operatives more than the pursuit of any

abstract principles. He fought the 1832 election in Leeds on factory questions, and relied on the upsurge of operative opinion in the Leeds neighbourhood between 1830 and 1832 as a "sort of antagonist irritation" to the Reform Bill campaign. . . .

In the light of this divergence between middle-class parliamentary reformers and working-class factory reformers, a key position was obviously held by working-class political reformers in the town. They formed a quite distinct group which had been created between 1819 and 1830, particularly by Mann, a bookseller who had previously been a cloth-dresser, and whose house as early as 1819 was described as "the headquarters of sedition in this town." They supported a political programme based on universal suffrage rather than an economic programme based on machine-breaking or strikes, for to build unions of trades was "only like lopping the branches of a cornel tree, leaving the corrupting root to strike forth with greater strength than before."

As late as September 1831 this radical group was prepared to devote most of its energies to the parliamentary reform question, and even to provide speakers on a common platform with the supporters of Baines. But Baines strongly disliked universal suffrage, the ballot and annual parliaments, which Mann and Foster, the two leading radicals, put into the forefront of their programme. At the first important meeting of the radicals on the eve of the crisis in September 1829, Baines, who was present, warned them not to meet in holes and corners, but to unite in a common cause with all other reformers. A few days later he pronounced them "wholly unfit to take the lead in the promotion of any great national measure." The operative radicals were fairly quiet from October 1829 to March 1830, although they maintained their newspaper, the *Leeds Patriot,* with Foster as editor, and offered long-distance support to the Birmingham Political Union. In February they attacked the limited reform, proposed by Russell, of separate repre-

sentation for Leeds, Manchester and Birmingham as an attempt "to divide the reformers generally and confer no benefits on
the people at large." In March they moved
amendments at a whig public meeting, and
in May they held a mass rally on Hunslet
Moor, and proposed the formation of a
Political Union, not on the lines of the
Birmingham Political Union, but on those
of the Metropolitan Political Union, with
an elected council of not more than fifty
members. The vicissitudes in the progress
of the Reform Bill through Parliament
brought them into some sort of rough-and-
ready agreement with the Leeds whigs, and
they appeared on the platform at the big
whig rally on 26 September 1831.

This was the last time, however, that
they were closely associated with the whigs.
When Hunt visited Leeds on 3 November
1831, he commended Sadler to the political
radicals despite his toryism, and claimed
that "he would be ten thousand times more
disposed to assist the working classes than
the briefless barrister Macaulay." A fort-
night later the radicals set up a distinctive
working-class Political Union, and from
the moment of its formation they interested
themselves as much in the Irish question
and the Ten Hours Bill[2] as in parliamentary reform. When the Grey government
fell in May 1832, instead of supporting the
fallen administration, they attacked it as a
coalition to deprive the operative classes of
all political influence for ever.

In the meantime, the Leeds tories more
than met the radicals half-way. As early as
March 1831, Baines wrote to his son of
Hunt's "flirtation" with the Reform Bill, and
claimed that "wonderful to be said, the
Honourable William Duncombe, one of
the (tory) members for Yorkshire, is of that
opinion." The tory Leeds Intelligencer held

out an open hand to the radicals, and Sadler himself went out of his way to meet
them. The Intelligencer claimed that "if
a still lower class of voters were admitted
under the Bill, Mr. Sadler's supporters
would be more than proportionately
increased."

The result of these tory-radical alignments and the alienation of local operatives
from the cause of parliamentary reform was
a bitter election contest in Leeds in December 1832. Macaulay and Marshall, the
whig candidates, were as violent in their
language as their single tory opponent, Sadler. If Marshall, the wealthy flax spinner,
was attacked as a capitalist, possessed of the
"mechanical power" which "crushed the
operatives, men, women and children to the
earth," Sadler was attacked by Macaulay as
"a convenient philanthropist," rather like
"a certain wild beast called the Hyaena
who, when it wishes to decoy the unwary
into its den, has a singular knack of imitating the cries of little children."

Despite the noise and bustle of the tory-
radical alliance in Leeds, the Whig £10
householders triumphed, polling heaviest
in the out-townships and saving themselves from becoming the laughing stock of
England by giving their votes at their first
election to Sadler, "the man who STROVE
TO PREVENT US HAVING ANY VOTES TO GIVE."
Although Sadler received 932 plumpers as
against Marshall's 20 and Macaulay's 21,
he was at the bottom of the poll.

The result of the election was a triumph
for the whigs, but it provoked interesting
tory reactions. At a dinner the tories gave
on 21 December, Sadler explained the defeat in terms of the narrowness of the new
franchise, which still excluded the operatives. "The people are entirely without
representation," he said. Oastler employed
the same theme at Wakefield on 20 December, when he denounced the £10 franchise,
and looked forward to a wider suffrage to
secure factory reform. He hoped that re-
juvenated toryism would have its part to
play in such a movement. "Now tories,
what say you? Will you join the whigs

[2] As early as 1830, Lord Ashley began his fight
for a ten-hour bill, a law which would limit the
work of all women and young people in factories
to no more than ten hours a day. The bill did not
apply to adult male workers, but it affected them
as well, for in many factories it was not practical
to have different shifts for the different sexes.
The bill passed in 1847. [Editor's note.]

against the people? If so you are a set of unprincipled knaves, and deserve to meet with the first reward of roguery. Will you go forward then with 'the people' and thus save the nation from anarchy and blood?" The Reform Bill had settled nothing, but it had provided a challenge. The challenge was not political but social, and the hope for the future lay not in abstractions, but in practical measures to deal with the condition of England.

In each of the three cities discussed in this article, there was a tendency for the local problem to colour the approach to reform politics — in Birmingham, currency; in Manchester, corn; in Leeds, machinery and the length of the working day. The alignments on these issues corresponded closely to the facts of local social structure, but successful change in each case demanded a national rather than a local remedy. In each city the demand for parliamentary reform was positive, in the sense that men asked clearly and with determination "What would parliamentary reform *do?*" As Molesworth pointed out in his *History of the Reform Bill,* written in 1865, "the clamour for reform sprang not so much from a sense of the theoretical imperfections of the then existing state of things" as from a sense of distress and an expectation of alleviation and improvement. Attwood expressed the same point of view in 1832 itself. "It was often said that it was the Duke's declaration against reform which drove him from office, but with this opinion he differed. It was at least the distress of the country which primarily led to the agitation of Reform, and had it not been for that, his Grace's declaration, however abrupt and unjustified, would have had no consequences. Distress was the cause — Reform the effect." Reform itself needed to be justified by its results. "The Reform Bill can no more rectify our ills than it can have caused them. It is from a different system after the Reform Bill is disposed of that we are to expect any improvement in our affairs."

Considered against such a background

of reform politics in these cities, the whig ministers in London appear not as masters of the situation, but merely as the temporary directors of it. They were anxious to acknowledge the place of trade and manufacture in a changing British economy by enfranchizing cities and towns which represented new interests, and to attach the middle classes to the established institutions of the country by making them consider the House of Commons as an ultimate tribunal where grievances could be discussed and remedied. When they talked in such terms and not in terms of traditional abstractions they were nearest to the opinion of the cities, but they were also submitting themselves to a subsequent scrutiny and a possible judgment. "With the people, the whigs may continue to rule," was a popular cry, "without them, they are doomed to destruction."

For the radicals, particularly the popular radicals, 1832 could not be a final measure. Within a year of the passing of the Act, while whigs in London talked of finality, Oastler was able to stir up Yorkshire, Doherty to build his General Union, and Attwood, basing his hopes on a million unemployed within the foreseeable future, to dream of vast new changes. Indeed, in 1836, when the succession of good harvests which favoured the whigs came to an end, Attwood was remarking:

Mr. Cobbett used to say, "I defy you to agitate a fellow with a full stomach." Nothing is more true. Men do not generally act from abstract principles, but from deep and unrewarded wrongs, injuries and sufferings. The people of England never came forward to advocate the abstract principles of Major Cartwright . . . but when they saw and felt that the yoke of the boroughmongers was laid heavy upon them they very easily and very quickly shook it off. When their employment and wages were gone and the boroughmongers stood convicted before the country, the boroughmongers were very quickly cashiered. Now when the next opportunity comes, a further reform of Parliament will be a much quicker and easier operation.

Reform and the Role of Interests

BLACKWOOD'S EDINBURGH MAGAZINE

Blackwood's Edinburgh Magazine first appeared in 1817. The early years are noted for the way in which its contributors contended against its opponents, particularly the Whigs and the London economists. It upheld a Scotch type of patriotic ultra-Toryism, expressed the view of the landowning class and defended the Protestant constitution in church and state. When there was a defection from their own narrow type of Toryism, its writers could be more critical of their own Tory leaders than the Whigs. On these occasions, *Blackwood's'* reporting was highly emotional and at times illogical. Prior to the introduction of the Whig reform bill, *Blackwood's* was reacting to Peel's apostacy on Catholic emancipation and was favorable to reform of Parliament. In this selection, *Blackwood's* shrewdly draws a distinction between the political aristocracy and the agricultural interest and argues that the borough influence, largely controlled by the aristocracy, operated to the detriment of the agricultural interest.

IT WOULD NOW be very unprofitable to enquire whether the House of Commons ought to be reformed; the die is cast; Reform is resolved on by both the Ministry and the Country, therefore the question for beneficial discussion is — what change ought to be adopted? . . . All parties have been long the avowed friends of Reform; even the Tories, who profess the most decided opposition to it, have still their own plan, to which they give its name; on their declarations, they, as well as the Radicals, are Reformers. . . .

The present system has long worked in the most baleful manner possible. When the Catholic Question was carried, it was proved that a coalition of the great borough interests could make almost any change of law and institution, in defiance of the public voice, and the solemn engagements of the Legislature. No upright man can say that this ought to remain without remedy. For several years the House of Commons has treated the sentiments and petitions of the community with the utmost disregard; and it has never even attempted to remove the unexampled public suffering which has prevailed without intermission. At present the House proclaims the population to be in great distress, yet it takes no statesmanlike view of causes, and proposes no adequate remedies; it contents itself with repeating, parrot-like, the vulgar, ignorant, factious cry for retrenchment and reduction of taxes, although every schoolboy knows that, in the nature of things, it is impossible for the latter to yield any relief worthy of notice to national loss and want. Thus it is proved by experience, that the present system forms a House of Commons which neither supplies proper security for public possessions, nor possesses the ability required for the discharge of its ordinary duties.

This system is so far from preventing change in the distribution of election power, that it is hourly making it. It is an argument with the anti-reformers, that reform would, of necessity, be revolution, because it would place power in new hands: now that which they defend, is continually producing the revolution they profess to oppose; it is constantly transferring power from the Aristocracy to the Democracy, and giving effect to the schemes of the Radicals. We need only point to late elections, and particularly the last one, for proof that in

Blackwood's Edinburgh Magazine, XXIX (February, 1831), pp. 235, 237–240, 242–243.

many open boroughs it has given the populace as complete an ascendency as universal suffrage could do; and that in various counties it has placed both the Aristocracy and Agriculture in the minority. These anti-reformers bewailed the issue of the last election, and yet it was produced by change of interest and person, but not of sentiment and conduct, in the elector; it was the natural and certain fruit of the system they defend. In the nature of things, the latter must regularly extend what is tantamount to universal suffrage amidst the boroughs, and enlarge the command of manufactures and trade over counties. If it make no direct change in the close boroughs, it makes a very sweeping indirect one; it destroys the means by which they work for good, combines them and degrades them into engines of vicious private gain.

This system causes an election war between the Aristocracy and the Democracy, which reform only can terminate. The lower orders, so far as principle is concerned, elect none but professed enemies of the former; and manufacturing and trading freeholders act in the same manner in counties. While it thus makes it the great object of the elector to return the most unfitting representative — to elect the demagogue and profligate, it of necessity carries the same war into the House of Commons, and makes it the great object of a large part of this House to sacrifice public interests for the sake of aspersing and trampling on the Aristocracy. The system, therefore, fills the mass of the people with disaffection, leads them to embrace the most pernicious principles of policy, and renders the popular branch of the Legislature an engine of discord and public ruin! . . .

The close boroughs form the great object of contention between the reformers and their opponents; the former attack, and the latter defend them, on the ground that they are possessed by the Aristocracy. Both sides err egregiously. The Aristocracy, as a whole, does not possess, and it draws little exclusive benefit from them. They belong to a few Peers and Commoners, who use them as individuals for private gain; and the great body of the Peers have no boroughs. On all matters which more directly affect the Aristocracy, for example, the Game and Corn Laws, it finds the close-borough members divided; and at the best, it has only the few votes which one division possesses more than the other. With the exception of a number too small to have any material effect on the general decisions of the House of Commons, the close boroughs practically belong as much to the Democracy as to the Aristocracy; their members act like those of the open ones.

When the history of late years is looked at, it seems a most ludicrous absurdity to argue that the close boroughs form a source of exclusive benefit to the Aristocracy as a body. The men who have regularly attacked the latter — who have continually taken the lead in depriving it of its possessions — who have made it the object of popular animosity — and who have, as even its enemies assert, placed it on the brink of destruction, have been the members of these close boroughs. It has found in these very boroughs the most bitter of its foes; it has suffered infinitely more from them than the rest of the community, and there is the best reason for believing that its situation would have been far better than it is, had they not been in existence.

The truth is, in general the Aristocrat who possesses a certain number attaches himself for private gain to the Ministry or Opposition; in consequence, they are not used for the benefit of the Aristocracy, but for that of party; they are made to operate like the open ones. In these days, when the popular side has gained the ascendency and the Ministry follow it, the close boroughs are in the majority used as a tremendous weapon against the Aristocracy.

The assertion that they give to the latter a monopoly of place, is not true; they only give it to a few individual aristocrats, to the prejudice of the Aristocracy as a body. Because the vicious and imbecile exception possesses them, the great mass of virtuous and talented Peers are as much excluded from office, as uninfluential commoners. . . .

The honest part of the Reformers are willing to spare a certain number of these boroughs as a means of admitting talent into the House of Commons. We apprehend there will be infinite difficulty in making this a matter of legal arrangement. The talent must not only be admitted, but it must be divided, and a full share of it must always be in opposition. The number might easily be fixed, but not the ownership. Although they are at present filled by the choice of party, they belong to individuals who frequently change sides. The Marquis of Cleveland is, we believe, a pretty large proprietor; this man has been, for some years, constantly leaping from side to side, with all the agility of a mountebank; and by extraordinary accident, some piece of personal benefit has fallen on himself at almost every leap. The Marquis of Hertford is, we think, another; he supported, in succession, the Liverpool, Canning, and Goderich cabinets, and he is now in opposition. Various of the great borough owners have, in late years, changed sides more than once, in violation of principle, and apparently from the base motive of private benefit. Mr. Canning, by the formation of his Ministry, and the Duke of Wellington and Sir R. Peel, by their conduct on the Catholic Question, wellnigh destroyed integrity amidst public men; and these borough owners have since taken the first place in exhibiting sordid and shameless disregard of it. A number of ministerial and opposition boroughs might be spared but it would be neither practicable nor proper to bind individual owners of them constantly to the same side. What Cleveland, or Hertford, or Bedford, or Rutland, could, in these liberal times, be always restricted to the bread and water of opposition? Without bonds, the opposition boroughs would, probably, be nearly all ministerial ones, a month after the passing of the Reform law. . . .

We do not speak thus for the sake of the Aristocracy; the distinction of the boroughs might, we believe, be effected without injuring its interests. We are anxious to see the abomination they form in principle removed; but, seeking nothing beyond reform, we are also anxious to retain the benefits they yield in operation. We cannot consent to sweep away good with evil. It is an easy matter to generalize, and if it were only necessary to look at the elector, reform might be understood by the factious dunces who decide on it so rashly. But impartial men who love their country will not be satisfied with merely glancing at the surface; they will not be moved by assertion and calumny; they will examine deeply and widely, and sanction such change alone as will be improvement. Either substitute for these boroughs something which will secure to the great leaders of opposition the easy and certain entrance into Parliament they have hitherto had, or, for the sake of liberty and the empire, preserve them with all their iniquity!

If they, or any part of them, be abolished, the question arises — to whom are their seats to be transferred? Putting out of sight the Aristocracy, they have always, in the most flourishing part of English history, belonged to the landed interest; and if nothing beyond reform be attempted, they must, after the abolition, belong to it. The name of this interest has, in late years, been as studiously suppressed, as though it had been without existence. The newspaper scribes and gin-shop reviewers have always spoken from motives alike guilty and obvious, as though the whole land of the country were held by the great Aristocrats. Placing the latter and their land entirely out of the question, there is a landed interest, which in wealth and numbers is of far greater importance than any other; and according to the constitution, justice and equity, it has as much right as any other to be represented in the House of Commons. Every honest reformer will say, that on the score of public good, the seats which are now its own, must not be taken from it by reform; how to secure them to it, requires much consideration.

This great interest in late years has been far more inefficiently represented than any other, the causes of this are continually enlarged, and without reform, the distress which has so long sat on it must soon become ruin.

In circumstance and system of election, other interests have a destructive superiority over it; and this is utterly indefensible, even on the uniformity doctrines of the Radicals. In the first place, while it has no influence in filling the seats of other interests, the latter have almost as much as itself in filling the only seats it possesses. The landowners have no share in electing the members of manufacturing and trading places; but the manufacturers and traders have a vast share in electing the members of counties; and they have lately gained the support of various borough owners. Small country towns which are open, are about as free from the influence of the landed interest as London and Liverpool; and their inhabitants are as hostile to it, as those of the manufacturing districts.

It follows that the members of manufactures and trade represent them only, and therefore they zealously promote their interests at the cost of agriculture, as the best means of securing their own re-election; but those of agriculture represent manufactures and trade likewise; in consequence they cannot, in many cases, even defend its interests, without ensuring their expulsion from their seats; probably of two county members, one regularly acts with its enemies, while the other opposes them with nothing better than compromise.

This state of things rapidly grows worse. The cities and boroughs continually become more independent of, and hostile to, the landed interest; and manufacturing and trading freeholders increase very greatly, while agricultural ones remain almost stationary. This interest has already been stripped of the county members in Middlesex and Surrey, and if no reform take place, it will soon share the same fate in various other counties. Its members are losing the seats for boroughs they formerly possessed; and not many of them can now afford to contest either borough or county. Not only manufacturers and merchants, but even trading lawyers and party empirics, aspire at present to county seats.

In the second place, the elective franchise in manufactures and trade is gained not only by purchase, but by birth, servitude, occupancy, and we think marriage: in agriculture it is gained only by property. In the former, mechanics, labourers, and petty tradesmen, to an enormous extent, have votes, independently of property of any kind; and in the latter, neither labourer nor farmer has a vote, if he have not a freehold of a certain value. In manufactures and trade, the poor voters go with the rich ones, and surpass them in hostility to agriculture; but the small and middling freeholders of country towns, are as much opposed to the latter, as those of large manufacturing places.

In the third place, a borough can be contested at far less cost than a county, and the latter cannot be contested on the side of agriculture, with any hope of success, without the support of certain great families. It follows that the borough has greater choice of members, and is represented with more ability and independence, than the county.

In the fourth place, the members of the landed interest are connected with the party Aristocracy; but those of other interests are not. If, therefore, Ministers decide on sacrificing it, they, by their influence with this Aristocracy, are enabled to array almost half its own members against it, and neutralize the whole. Although this interest has a great number of members, it is little better than nominally represented; it is at the mercy of government; on every emergency, one party of them by their dependence on trade and manufactures, on the one hand, and the party Aristocrats on the other, make the whole powerless in its favour. If trade and manufactures be attacked, their members act unanimously and independently in their defence.

And in the fifth place, government has been for some time acting on the policy of basing itself more and more on trade and manufactures, and conciliating them by inroads on agriculture — the great party aristocrats are ranging themselves more and more with trade and manufactures — the latter are carrying on a war of extermination against agriculture, and both the Ministry and Opposition have embraced the doctrine, that its continual, though gradual, sacrifice to them, is necessary for the common good.

From all this, our own most carefully formed and conscientious opinion is, that the Landed Interest and Aristocracy, as a whole, have only this choice before them — Reform or ruin. It is demonstrated by experience, and the nature of things, that the present system will soon virtually drive them out of the House of Commons, and render them defenceless against the mighty enemies who seek to plunge them into destruction.

III. SOME CONSEQUENCES OF THE REFORM BILL

The Social Composition of the Parliament of 1833

S. F. WOOLLEY

S. F. Woolley (born July 31, 1905) was formerly headmaster of the Elmfield County Secondary School, Morley, Leeds. His "Personnel of the Parliament of 1833," published in 1938 in the *English Historical Review*, is an early statistical study of the post-Reform Bill House of Commons. Woolley emphasizes the extremely slight difference which the Reform Bill made with regard to the class of member sitting in the House of Commons. He concludes that the business interests had greater representation prior to 1832 than they had in the Parliament of 1833, and that the landed gentry and the landed aristocracy continued to represent the counties in which they resided.

THERE ARE NO adequate grounds for asserting, as some have done, that parliamentary representation was fundamentally changed by the Reform Act of 1832. The object of the present article is to estimate, more precisely than has been done heretofore, its effects on parliamentary personnel, that is to compare the membership of the parliament which met in 1833 with that of previous parliaments.

One common opinion, which must at all events be regarded as illusory by all those familiar with eighteenth-century parliamentary history, is that the industrial north, with its large rising towns, had no one to represent it in parliament before 1832. True, very few of the northern towns were parliamentary boroughs, but their manufacturers and merchants managed to find seats in the house of commons. . . . As the eighteenth century wore on, the men of trade increased their numbers in the house of commons until in 1832 they formed a fairly considerable phalanx. Many of them gained their entry by the purchase of boroughs. . . .

One definite and important change was wrought by the Reform Act of 1832. Many members who had sat for rotten boroughs were now elected for their counties or for boroughs near which they lived. This especially applied to the country gentlemen owing to the increase of the county membership of England and Wales from 94 to 159. . . . The question arises how far the Act of 1832 affected the numbers of the mercantile class in parliament. Did it cause an immediate increase in their representation? Certainly the reformed parliament showed a more decided change in personnel than was usual, but there was no unprecedented influx of the middle classes. Another problem to be determined is the extent to which the new borough constituencies like Leeds, Birmingham, and Lambeth, elected members of a character entirely different from those who sat for the older boroughs. Were these new constitu-

From S. F. Woolley, "Personnel of the Parliament of 1833," *English Historical Review,* LIII (1938), pp. 240–252, 254–256, 259–261. Reprinted by permission of the author.

encies content with the members of the old political families, with the aristocracy and landed gentry as their representatives in parliament, or did they embark on a new line, preferring men of their own class who had little or no parliamentary experience? . . .

In the *Parliamentary Pocket Book* for 1833 the number of new members is given as 277 for the whole parliament, and 186 for the constituencies of England and Wales. My own figures, however, founded on a careful examination of the official *Return of Members of Parliament,* are still less, being 252 new members (i.e. members who had never sat before) for the whole parliament and 184 for England and Wales. When it is considered that the new members for England and Wales in the parliament of 1826 were 135, i.e. 26 per cent as against 37 per cent in 1833, the contrast, after all, between 1826 and 1833 in respect of personnel is not so startling, whilst in succeeding parliaments the normal change was quickly resumed, there being 184 new men for all constituencies (England, Wales, Scotland, and Ireland) in the parliament of 1835, and 158 in 1837.

One reason why the 1833 parliament did not show a greater "landslide" is that to a certain degree the change of personnel had already taken place in the elections of 1830 and 1831. The government party, composed of Whigs, Canningites, and ultra-Tories, had a majority in parliament as a result of the election of 1830, small though that majority was shown to be by the voting on the Gascoyne amendment. But this slight majority was considerably augmented at the election of 1831 as the divisions in the commons over the reform measure clearly indicate. It was unlikely that an electorate that had witnessed the passing of the Reform Bill would fail to return those Whig members who had shown themselves willing to enlarge the franchise. The fact that there was already a powerful Whig majority in the parliament of 1831 must be taken into account when considering the change of personnel in 1833.

In some ways there is scope for the comparison of the reformed house of commons of 1833 with that of 1831. Each was elected in a time of crisis, in each there was an overwhelming majority in favour of the government, and each involved a much greater change in personnel than was usual at elections. The opposition party of 1833 was, however, not so utterly crushed as that of 1831. Even the *Annual Register* felt compelled to announce that "it was surprising that the Tories carried so many seats." In point of fact, as Croker had predicted in a letter to Lord Fitzgerald on 28 August 1832, they carried 150 seats. The precise balance of parties in the first parliament is not easy to assess numerically on account of the changing politics of certain members, more especially those middle-class Radicals who later came to identify themselves with the Whigs. The newspapers and other contemporary periodicals, however, seem to be more or less agreed on the state of the parties. A survey of the strength of the parties is printed in the *Spectator,* and gives the ministerialists a clear majority over their Tory opponents of 364, i.e. 511 as against 147. J. S. Buckingham, the Radical member for Sheffield, provides almost identical figures but classifies them thus: 150 Conservatives, 408 Whigs, 96 Liberals, and 4 Independents. It is impossible, however, to accept the number of Liberals or Radicals as final, for 17 of them were Irish members, and a fair percentage of the remainder were very moderate in their opinions and soon came to be completely merged in the ranks of the Whig party.

As a matter of fact, one of the most disappointing features of the reformed parliament, from the point of view of the middle and lower middle classes, was the comparative fewness of the Radical members returned and the essential moderation of the parliament as a whole. Creevey, in a letter to Miss Ord, writes:

It seems made perfectly manifest by their vote that the Reform Parliament is not a Radical one, when Joe Hume and the Right Hon. Tennyson and all the O'Connells and all the Repealers with Cobbett to boot, could only muster 40 against 400!

At the same time, though few in numbers, the Radicals were destined to exert considerable influence upon social reform and upon political thought. More especially does this apply to that small group known as the "Philosophical Radicals," who for the most part were the advocates of Benthamite teachings. Joseph Hume, who had sat in parliament since 1812, might be regarded as the leader of this group, but to it were now added several young and brilliant members, notably, Sir William Molesworth, returned for the Eastern Division of Cornwall, John Arthur Roebuck, George Grote, banker and historian and member for London, Charles Buller, and John Romilly. Amongst these men of ideas must also be included Edward Lytton Bulwer, the novelist, and his brother, Henry Bulwer.

Another feature of the parliament likely to cause comment was the almost negligible number of nonconformist members. It has been estimated that in every borough election of 1832 the nonconformists formed the backbone of the majority, yet the fewness of the nonconformist representatives in 1833 is almost disconcerting. Apart from the unitarians, of whom there were six — G. W. Wood, Brotherton, Harvey, Faithfull, Dillon, and Fielden — only two members of the dissenting sects sat in the first reformed parliament. They were John Pease, a quaker, and John Wilks, a methodist, to whom was added later at a by-election Edward Baines, a congregationalist.

In spite of their opposition to reform, the ranks of the Tories as we have seen, were by no means so much depleted as had been anticipated by many of the less acute observers. However much this may be ascribed to the continuance of the practice of open voting, and the consequent bribery and intimidation, it is not possible to account for it without some reference to the inher-

ent loyalty of the British electorate to certain members of the old governing families. It must, of course, be conceded that not all the Tories were diametrically opposed to change. Even an ultra-Tory like Lord Hertford was not averse to some measure of reform. He, together with others of his group, took the common-sense view that, reform being inevitable, it would have been wiser "to give up a part to save some part"; and it must be remembered that Wellington had his chance to introduce a moderate reform in November 1830, but preferred "to slide out of office on the Civil List" rather than face it. He made matters worse by eulogizing the British constitution as the most perfect that the human mind could devise. This speech not merely served to fan popular indignation, but failed in any object it might have had of re-uniting the disparate groups within the Tory ranks. Lord Hertford, writing to Croker from Milan, censures the duke on this point: "I regretted the Duke's sweeping denial of change, not as bad in itself, but as unwise and unnecessary, as it did not even secure the rejunction of the Tories. . . ." In actual fact, a group of Tories in the house of lords, known as "the Waverers" and led by Lords Harrowby and Wharncliffe, by voting for the second reading of the third reform measure, materially helped to secure the passage of the bill. The Tory minority in the new house, moreover, was a substantial one, containing many of the old faces. That Peel was returned for Tamworth, Goulburn for the University of Cambridge, Herries for Harwich, Charles Wynn for Montgomeryshire, and Hardinge for Launceton, causes no surprise, for they were leaders of the party; but among the 150 Tories were some of the bitterest opponents of the Reform Bill, such as Alexander Baring, who was elected for the Northern Division of Essex, and Sir Richard Vyvyan, the member for Bristol.

The gloomiest forebodings of the effects of the Reform Bill were contained in many contemporary periodicals, and not the least of these effects was the change in personnel that was bound to occur.

Station, property, education, professional eminence, political experience, local connexion — nay, personal talents — "will pale their ineffectual lights" before the devouring conflagration, however it may be kindled by popular excitement.

This was a characteristic view and was largely responsible for causing many nineteenth-century writers to assume that the Reform Act did actually produce a violent change. But the late Élie Halévy indicated in 1923 with some emphasis the extremely slight, almost imperceptible, difference which the Reform Act made to the class of member sitting in parliament. He writes:

After 1832, the House of Commons, we might suppose, would be suddenly filled with financiers, merchants and manufacturers. Nothing of the kind took place. The number of business men in the House remained after 1832 practically the same as before.

In an appendix to the Black Book (1834) considerable attention is directed to the personnel of the first reformed parliament: "If we look to the composition of the lower house, we shall find that what may be termed the aristocratic interests have still a numerical preponderance." A classification is given, and, after emphasizing the fact that 151 members were united by ties of consanguinity with members of the house of lords (73 were sons of peers and 78 others related to the peerage), the Black Book states: "It is worthy to be remarked that in the house are only 49 merchants, manufacturers, and traders." There were also, according to the Black Book, 71 lawyers, 64 officers of the army, 19 holding naval commissions, 45 officers in the militia and yeomanry, 75 members who had church patronage, and 60 members who held offices and received emoluments from civil appointments, pensions, and sinecures. These figures do not seem to have been seriously challenged, and most writers of the period appear to have arrived at similar results.

The *Assembled Commons,* a pamphlet published in 1838, gives precisely the same numbers regarding the army and navy officers, and further adds that 400 members followed no profession, whilst 200 were relatives or clients of peers.

In several parliaments prior to 1833, the number of merchants was equal, if not superior, to that of the first reformed parliament. For example, in the parliament of 1830 there were 62 members connected with the East India interest, 35 with the West India interest, and 33 who were bankers. Of the same parliament, William Carpenter, in a *Political Letter* dated 6 November 1830, states that there were 82 merchants and traders, and 36 bankers. Statistics for the parliament of 1831, the last before the Reform Act came into operation, also show that the proportion of the business element was then perceptibly greater than in the first reformed parliament. *The Parliamentary Record* (1833) classifies the interests in the last unreformed parliament as follows: landholders 358, military officers 88, naval officers 24, bankers 33, East India Interest 62, West India Interest 34, General Trade 51, profession of the law 62, placemen and pensioners 63. Allowing for a certain overlapping of interests, the merchants and traders will thus be seen to form a not inconsiderable element in the parliament of 1831, and when it is realized that there were 98 sons of peers sitting in this parliament as against 73 in 1833, there are some grounds for a retort made by Baring during a debate on the Reform Bill. The reformers were arguing that the unreformed parliament was insensible to the wishes of the people, whereupon Baring was said to have exclaimed, "Si monumentum quaeris — circumspice! [If you are looking for evidence — just look around you]. . . ."

The result of the redistribution of seats and the changes in the franchise made by the Reform Act was that England had 144 county members, representing 344,564 registered electors, and 327 borough members (including those for the two universities), representing 274,649 electors; Wales had 15 county members, representing 25,815 electors, and 14 borough members, representing 11,309 electors; Scotland had 30 county members to 33,114 electors, and 23 borough members to 31,332 electors; Ireland had 64 county members to 60,607 electors, and 41 borough members to 31,-545 electors: in the United Kingdom there were thus 253 county and 405 borough members, representing 464,100 and 348,-835 members respectively. The relative strength of the county and borough representations—an unmistakable feature of these figures—aroused much comment at the time:

The first remark that occurs is upon the proportion of the town to the county suffrage. In round numbers, the gross population of the cities and boroughs of England and Scotland is half the population of the counties; and the representation of the cities and boroughs is about double the representation of the counties. Wales gives advantage to the counties; and the returns for Great Britain stand thus:

	Population	Members
County	10,446,241	189
Borough	5,816,060	364

so that the county population is two to one against the town and the town representatives two to one against the county. [*Black Book,* 1834]

The view that the boroughs were greatly over-represented at the expense of the counties was one of the strongest and bitterest Tory criticisms of the Reform Act, as is readily comprehensible when it is considered that the strength of the Tories lay with the landed interest, their weakness in the large manufacturing towns. . . . The *Quarterly Review* of 1835 stated quite categorically that the Whig's cry for "a better representation in parliament" was only pretence but that their real object was "the transfer of power from the Tories to the Whigs. . . . The destruction of all nomination boroughs was their profession — the overthrow of Tory nomination, and the

maintenance and extension of Whig nomination their intention." This is undoubtedly an exaggeration, and while it may be that some of the Whigs allowed weight to their party interests, it would be unjust to say that their motives in passing the Reform Bill were entirely selfish. They did, at any rate, grasp what most of the Tories failed to see, that political reform was inevitable. They made mistakes, but in so great a task, mistakes were bound to occur. On the face of it they did appear to be giving a predominant influence — at least numerically — to the boroughs, but the Reform Bill was no act of political suicide on their part, for they still maintained the system of open voting despite considerable agitation for a secret ballot, and, in regard to the borough franchise, there were wide differences in the number of voters. . . .

Although 56 small English boroughs were abolished in 1832, candidates recommended by the great landowners were still elected in many borough constituencies, in preference to independent ones, and there is little doubt that this was partly due to the system of open voting. The second great reason for the ease with which voters could be influenced lay in the comparative fewness of the electors in many boroughs even after 1832. For example, of the English and Welsh boroughs at the elections of 1832, seven polled less than 200, sixteen between 200 and 300, nineteen polled between 300 and 400, ten between 400 and 500, forty-two between 500 and 1000, twenty-two between 1000 and 2000, eight between 2000 and 3000, and twelve only above 3000, one of these being London which returned four members. The 86 representatives of the boroughs with an electorate of over 1000 formed 22½ per cent of the urban representation. These figures are indicative of change when compared with eighteenth-century parliaments. Thus, in the parliament of 1761, 22 English boroughs had an electorate of 1000, 22 between 500 and 1000, and 11 had each about 500 voters. This marked difference may indeed be accounted for partly by the unprecedented increase of population, a fact that must receive added significance when the figures for the unreformed parliaments of the nineteenth century are considered. The late M. Halévy concluded from his analysis of the borough franchise of England for the year 1815 that 30 boroughs possessed an electorate exceeding 1000, eight of them being scot and lot boroughs and 22 freemen boroughs.

A surprising feature of the election of 1832 is the fact that of the English and Welsh boroughs 54 were uncontested, including six of the new boroughs — Birmingham, Cheltenham, Gateshead, Kendal, Wakefield, and Merthyr Tydvil. In the counties the proportion was even greater. The 52 counties were divided for electoral purposes into 80 constituencies, and of these 32 were uncontested. That there were contests in 48 constituencies serves to show the freedom of elections after 1832, especially since Professor Namier has demonstrated that contests in the counties for membership of the eighteenth-century parliaments were the exception. Even so, in the special circumstances in 1832 — the unsettled state of the country and the general effects of reform — the return of so many country representatives without contest implied not merely continuity of loyalty, but possibly, with the electoral structure as it was then, of influence (called nomination prior to the Reform Act).

The aristocratic influence was strong in the counties and in those small boroughs where the voters were few and therefore more easily affected by the local landowners. Naturally, there was some displacement in view of the excited state of the public at the time, but the landed gentry quickly resumed their sway. To quote a nineteenth-century writer: "England is governed in times of excitement by her people, in quiet times by her property," and such a statement was never more fully borne out than in the case of the county constituencies and the older borough constituencies. Ninety-seven of the 144 members, who represented the English counties in the first reformed parliament, had sat before; of these, 15 had sat in parliaments before 1831 but not actually in the parliament of that year, 64 had represented counties, 10 disfranchised boroughs, and 8 had sat for boroughs which had survived the passing of the Reform Bill. There were, of course, a few bankers, lawyers, and merchants amongst the county members such as John Smith, a banker and member for Buckinghamshire, Edward Stillingfleet Cayley, a lawyer representing the North Riding of Yorkshire, and Thomas Houldsworth, the cotton manufacturer who sat for the Northern Division of Nottinghamshire, but the overwhelming majority were of the landowning class. . . .

There is no direct evidence that the Whigs wilfully manipulated the Reform Act. They continued to assert that population was not the sole basis on which the distribution of seats had been allotted, that so far as the boroughs had been concerned, a mixed test had been applied, the Reform Committee being guided by the number of persons in a borough, the number of houses, and the amount of assessed taxes. As a result of the application of this test, there were twelve disfranchised towns which had a population over 2000, and five half-disfranchised towns which had a population over 5000. Actually, there was only one way to meet the objections of Tories and Radicals alike on the point of the disfranchisement of small boroughs and the enfranchisement of large ones, and that was to adopt the principle of equal electoral districts. As long as the borough representation was maintained within the county, anomalies were bound to occur; but the Tories would have been the first people to rise up against the abolition of the traditional boroughs, the retention of which they knew to be greatly to their advantage.

To take next the boroughs which were half-disfranchised in 1832, 22 of the 60 members who had sat in 1831 for these boroughs found seats in the new parliament. The *Quarterly Review* bitterly attacks Schedule B as comprising the boroughs, *par excellence,* where nomination was still allowed to persist, and it brings in support of this, the fact that 17 out of the 30 constituencies were uncontested, "affording a pretty strong presumption that Schedule B is . . . still strongly tainted with nomination." It errs rather badly when it states that Calne, Midhurst, and Morpeth "returned without contest, the same persons — all reformers — that they did in the days of avowed nominations." As a matter of fact, the members were different, although one of them, Frederick George Howard, who sat for Morpeth, belonged to the same great territorial family which had represented it in the previous parliament. . . .

Finally, 26 members of the disfranchised boroughs represented other constituencies in the first reformed parliament, nearly half being returned for counties in which they had landed possessions, and the remainder for boroughs with which they had personal associations, and in which they could exercise family influence. A further 22, although not elected in 1832, had seats in subsequent parliaments, and they too, for the most part, represented constituencies near their homes. For example, George Bankes, a substantial Dorset squire who sat for the family borough of Corfe Castle till it was disfranchised, re-entered parliament as a member for the county in 1841; Philip John Miles, a merchant, also a member for Corfe Castle before 1832, was returned in 1835 for Bristol where he had carried on his business for many years. Thus even of the members for disfranchised boroughs, it cannot be maintained that an overwhelming majority was permanently excluded from parliament.

Most of the 111 members of the disfranchised boroughs were country gentlemen and relatives of the peerage, but 22 were of the mercantile class. This is a much higher percentage of merchants and bankers than in the parliament of 1831 taken as a whole, and indicates that the boroughs disfranchised in 1832 had provided the easiest means to a merchant of acquiring a seat in parliament. Six only of these 22 merchants and bankers — Staunton, Hope, Houldsworth, Henry Baring, Matthias Attwood, and William Miles — sat in the parliament of 1833; a most surprising result when it is considered that one of the avowed objects of the Reform Bill was to extend political power to the middle classes. Another six did manage to secure representation in later parliaments; they were Philip John Miles, Farrand, George Richard Philips, Abel Smith, Irving, and Bouverie — three of them, Philips, Smith, and Bouverie being closely related with the peerage. Thus, the disfranchisement of the fifty-six small boroughs, whatever may have been said of its aim, removed one of the most convenient means by which a merchant could use his wealth for political purposes.

Moreover, it may well be the case that a good many members of disfranchised boroughs did not stand for re-election in 1832 because they were apprehensive that, "a complete revolution is near at hand, and that property must every day become less secure. . . ." Such opinions were expressed by Croker, Raikes, and others, and must have been generally held by the upper classes, and especially by the Tories. Croker was invited to stand at the election of 1832 by the electors of Ipswich and of Wells, but he refused to do so, ostensibly on principle, though he may also have been influenced by knowledge that his health was impaired. He maintained his decision to retire from public life unswervingly; others, preferring not to engage in what they expected would be a severe and hotly-contested parliamentary election, refused to stand in 1832, but returned to parliament at the next election after observing what little change had actually taken place. . . .

The manufacturers, merchants, and bankers form the largest section of the members of the new borough constituencies, totalling 30, that is, over 46 per cent. The remaining 35 members were composed of 13 of the legal profession, 12 of the landed gentry, 5 army officers and 3 naval officers, and 2 journalists. One feature of the new borough elections, likely to arouse comment, was the number of representatives who were connected with the peerage. Despite the fact that the middle class electorate was comparatively large in the new boroughs and therefore less inclined to be influenced by the old aristocratic families, at least thirteen of the members elected were related in some way with the peerage. Most of these members were reformers or at least professed to be such, but it is a sign of the pronounced influence of the old ruling families that electors, having their first chance to vote, preferred to send back representatives of exactly the same calibre as before. . . .

The results of our whole investigation do nothing to upset the verdict of Greville on the first session of the reformed parliament:

The session is over, and a Reformed Parliament turns out to be very much like every other Parliament, except that it is rather differently and somewhat less ably composed than its predecessors. The hopes and fears of mankind have been equally disappointed, and after all the clamour, confusion, riots, conflagrations, furies, despair, and triumphs through which we have arrived at this consummation, up to the present time, at least, matters remain pretty much as they were, except that the Whigs have got possession of the power which the Tories have lost.

Social Composition and Interests in the Parliament of 1841–1847

WILLIAM O. AYDELOTTE

William O. Aydelotte (born 1910) is Chairman of the History Department, University of Iowa. The author of *Bismarck and British Colonial Policy* (1937), he has published significant articles on quantification in history in the *American Historical Review* (1966), *Journal of British Studies* (1966), *English Historical Review* (1967), *Comparative Studies in Society and History* (1963) and has contributed appendices to Norman Gash's *Reaction and Reconstruction in English Politics, 1832–1852* (1965) and G. Kitson Clark's *The Making of Victorian England* (1962). In this essay, Aydelotte uses a statistical approach "to cast light on such intricate and difficult problems as the social composition of parliament, the overlapping of different social and economic groups, and the relation of party, social position and economic interest to voting behaviour."

THIS PROJECT is a statistical study of the slightly over 800 men who sat in the house of commons between the general election of 1841 and the general election of 1847. An attempt has been made to assemble for all these men biographical information that could be tabulated and compared, something along the lines suggested by Professor Neale in his paper read at this conference three years ago, a paper which I did not, however, see until two years after it was delivered and long after I had begun this research. This project is in any case somewhat different and departs from the letter if not from the spirit of Professor Neale's blueprint in three respects. First, it has proved possible to obtain and to subject to statistical analysis a far greater variety of information than he suggests or than would probably be possible for any century before the nineteenth. Data have now been collected for most of the men in the 1841–47 parliament covering, among other things: party, type, location and size of constituency; location of residence; relation of residence to constituency; previous parliamentary experience; age in 1841 when this parliament opened; age at first entry into parliament; marital status in 1841 and 1847; relation to peerage, baronetage and landed gentry, both by descent and by marriage; date of creation of family title; business interests and professional activities (both of these in great detail); business interests and professional activities of father; education, both public school and university; clubs; local offices; and amount of railroad investment in 1845 and in 1846. Second, an attempt has been made to study not only biographical facts but also attitudes on various issues by means of a tabulation of the votes of these men in a total of 267 selected divisions in the house of commons. This information is arranged so that it can be correlated with biographical data, and thus it can readily be ascertained how various social, economic and other groups voted on particular issues at different times. In the third place, mechanical devices, punch-cards and IBM machines, have been used to sort and count the data more accurately and far more rapidly than could be done

From William O. Aydelotte, "The House of Commons in the 1840's," *History*, **XXXIX** (1954), pp. 249–262. Reprinted by permission of the author and the editor of *History*.

by hand. The use of mechanical aids has made it possible to plan a rather ambitious programme of correlation and systematic analysis.

The biographical information was originally recorded on 4 in. by 6 in. cards, about five for each man, and the votes were recorded on special sheets designed for that purpose. All this information has since been twice transferred, first to coded worksheets, and second and finally to IBM punch-cards. The collection of the information and its arrangement in a form in which it could be used statistically have been immensely laborious tasks.

The interest that has prompted this study has not been simply a desire to produce a statistical description of a parliament, though that of course has value in itself. I have also been concerned with wider issues, and have hoped that it might prove possible to use this detailed and systematically arranged information to verify certain general hypotheses on which there has been a singular amount of shifting of opinion or of outright disagreement. To take a few illustrations — not quite at random, for I wish to discuss these points presently — it is hard in the present state of knowledge to say precisely what is the accepted answer to any of the following rather significant questions:

1. How extensively had "middle class" or "business" elements penetrated into parliament by the 1840's? (Earlier historians have suggested that they were rapidly taking over political control; the more recent trend is to emphasize the survival of eighteenth-century aristocratic habits of government into the middle of the nineteenth century.)

2. How far did these elements constitute a distinct group, clearly separate from the landed interest? (Some historians stress the battle between the landed and business elements, which is said to have amounted almost to a class war in the 1840's; other historians stress the overlapping between these two groups.)

3. What social and economic groups were most prominent in each of the various parties? (Statements on this subject have also been at variance, in a manner that it would take too long to recapitulate.)

4. To what extent was economic reform, legislation on the condition-of-the-people question, supported or opposed by Conservatives, Whigs or Liberals; and to what extent was it supported or opposed by aristocrats or businessmen, and how far did people vote according to their own class or economic interests, narrowly construed? (While Whigs and Tories have both in their turn been cited as the authors of reform, the fashionable emphasis at the moment seems to be on the Conservative and aristocratic aspect of social legislation, which is thought to have been initiated by Conservatives and opposed by Liberals, initiated by land and opposed by business, each of these last two groups following in a general way its own economic interests. Yet this interpretation is often hedged with qualifications, and it is hard to state with certainty the present scholarly position.)

To most of these general questions there are possible at least two alternative and opposing answers and in the fullness of time, with historians correcting each other and the wheel coming full circle, both answers have generally been given. It is hard for any new interpretation to come as a surprise because almost every possible interpretation has already been suggested. The important thing, of course, is to discover, not what is surprising, but what actually happened.

To point to the variations of opinion is not to disparage earlier writers who in their own day made impressive contributions. On the contrary, most of these views, contradictory as they may be, contain a substantial amount of truth, and would scarcely have been accepted by reputable scholars if they had not. The evidence points both ways, and illustrations can be found for almost any thesis. The point is rather, and this is the crux of the argument, that in issues of this kind we are not dealing with absolutes. Such general statements are never wholly true but only partly true, and the point to raise about them is not "Whether?" but "How much?" These are quantitative questions and they are to be answered not by a dogma but by a percentage or ratio.

In solving large and general problems of this kind a statistical method can be of some advantage. Though it seems at first glance arid and forbidding, it can offer new insights that are stimulating and refreshing, and it can provide a reliable and exact basis for generalization. Yet it has drawbacks. Since it is a quantitative method it cannot reflect qualitative things, the intensity of an affiliation or the influence of an individual, except by translating these into quantitative terms, which in a study so involved as this it is not always practicable to do. Furthermore, anyone who has worked closely with his materials must be conscious that as soon as he begins to sort men into categories he is departing from reality. General labels are never accurate or satisfactory: they obscure important differences and describe only partially circumstances that are complex and varied.

Besides this, there are the practical difficulties of assembling the information and deciding how to interpret it. One might suppose that the statistical analysis of a parliament would be, though a laborious task, yet a relatively uncomplicated one, and that all that is needed is simply to get the facts and count them. But this is not so easy. In the first place it is more difficult than anyone who has not worked on a similar project would credit to assemble uniform and highly detailed information about 800 men who lived a century ago and many of whom were relatively obscure. Though there is much material, almost no major source is free from error, the sources are not comparable but provide different kinds of information and describe situations existing at different times, and there are unexpected gaps which in some cases cannot be filled. To get detailed information in a form that can be tabulated about all or even about most of these men is little less than a *tour de force*. Even greater are the difficulties of interpreting the information and making it meaningful in terms of the existing hypotheses which it is desired to test. The his-

tory of the period has been told in a language including such vague concepts of social differentiation as aristocrat and businessman, gentry and middle class. These expressions may have some general significance and they perhaps resemble, at least in their imprecision, the shadowy, fluid and sometimes illogical character of English class boundaries in the nineteenth century. Yet it is hard to transform such words, worn and slippery as they have become from loose and varied usage, into the firm and precise tools needed for exact research, or even to define them in terms of the detailed data. I am unable to say what kinds or amounts of economic interest make a man a "businessman" or how a member of the "landed gentry" may be reliably defined in any way other than by his inclusion in the edition of Burke's *Landed Gentry* that is contemporary to this parliament.

For these various reasons it seems clear that anyone who claims to have gathered complete and reliable social and economic data in a study of this character has simply not grappled with the problems. Any such figures must inevitably contain a certain amount of conjecture and, in consequence, a certain margin of error. Since statistics tend to lull the unwary into a false sense of security, it is all the more necessary that these reservations should be stated as frankly and plainly as possible.

During the lifetime of the parliament of 1841–47 a total of 815 men sat in the house of commons. About one-third of them (31%) had never sat in parliament before, about one-third (34%) had sat before the first reformed parliament assembled in 1833, and the remaining one-third (35%) entered parliament in the time between. More than half of them (56%) were in 1841 under 45 years old. In general they entered parliament at a much younger age: half of them (53%) had entered parliament before the age of 35, and a third of them (36%) before the age of 30. Of those whose marital status I know, approximately four-fifths were married by the year of the opening of this parliament, 1841, and one-fifth were bachelors. There were 151 bachelors, of whom 34 married during the lifetime of this parliament. Of those whose residence I know, 42% resided in their constituencies, another 26% represented boroughs located in counties in which they had residences, while 32% lived away from their constituencies altogether. Nearly half (46%) had attended a public school and about three-fifths (59%) had attended a university. Of those attending a university, over half (53%) had gone to Oxford, and a third (32%) to Cambridge.

To turn to a larger issue, it might be of interest to see what light this method of analysis can throw on the first of the problems I raised earlier, the social composition of the house. The question is: how far had a new social group which was distinct from the landed interest and which has been variously referred to as the "newer interests," the "middle classes" or the "businessmen" secured a place in the membership of this parliament?

In the first place, it is clear from the detailed figures that this parliament was heavily dominated, in numbers at least, by the nobility, baronetage and landed gentry and their relatives. In it there sat 8 Irish peers, 172 sons of peers (this figure includes 9 sons of Scottish peers, 11 sons of Irish peers, some illegitimate but acknowledged sons of peers and several men who had received the precedence of peers' sons by royal warrant), 27 grandsons and great-grandsons of peers, 82 baronets, 46 sons of baronets, 7 grandsons and great-grandsons of baronets, and 240 men who belonged by direct line of male descent to families listed in the contemporary Burke's Landed Gentry. All these men together constituted 71% of the membership of parliament and if those related through mother or wife were also included the figure would be 80%. Whether the figure of 71% exactly represents the aristocratic or landed class is of course open to some discussion. A number of the baronets were of recent creation — 15 of the 82 had received their titles from Queen Victoria — and it may not be meaningful to group such men with the nobility and gentry. On the other hand approximately half

of the baronets had titles dating back before 1800, and about half the sons of baronets came from families of equal antiquity. Furthermore, some of the nineteenth-century baronetcies were held by such obviously aristocratic figures as Sir George Grey (who was also the grandson of a peer), Sir Edward Kerrison and Sir William George Hylton Jolliffe. One cannot dismiss a baronetcy, as some of the novelists of the period did, as the distinction of the middle class. Another point that may slightly distort the results is that the edition of Burke's Landed Gentry which appeared at the end of this parliament and which has been used as the criterion of membership in the "landed gentry" did not include a number of men who seem to have lived the lives and enjoyed the prestige of country gentlemen, and who were included in later editions of this work. For these and other reasons the exact number of the landed or aristocratic group in this parliament can probably never be precisely settled. My own view is that the above estimate should, if anything, be revised upward. In any case, there can be no question about the fact that this parliament was overwhelmingly aristocratic in composition.

On the other hand, the role of business in this parliament proves on analysis to have been relatively modest. The kernel of the business group were 54 manufacturers, 64 men who called themselves merchants, and 32 partners in private banks, adding up, when the overlappings are cancelled out, to a total of 123 men. There were 122 directors of insurance companies and 145 railway directors, but most of these appear not to have been engaged full-time in business activities. The total of all the entries in all the 18 categories of economic interest that have been set up is 663, but there was a good deal of overlapping and these 663 business interests were divided among only 334 men, nearly two apiece. These 334 men represent 41% of the membership of parliament and there were 481 men, or 59%, who, so far as I have yet discovered, had no business interests whatsoever.

Furthermore, it seems clear that not all

of these 334 men can fairly be called "businessmen." Whatever meaning may be attached to that indefinite and unsatisfactory word, it would appear to signify at least some kind of a role in society in which business enterprise played a major part. However, many of these business interests made only minor demands on a man's time, and presumably also on his emotional allegiance, and would in no way conflict with his being principally committed to quite a different social role. It seems unrealistic to hold that being a director in a railway company or an insurance company necessarily placed a man in a position equivalent to that of a manufacturer, a merchant, or a partner in a private bank.

It is unprofitable to inquire what particular kinds of economic interest make a man a businessman, for the expression is inexact and the duties of men in almost any kind of economic enterprise may differ. I estimate that the number of those actively engaged in the operation or control of major business enterprises, including proprietors and chairmen but not including those who were merely directors or who were only incidentally concerned, was 179 or 22% of the membership of parliament. While this estimate can be only a rough one, it will at least help to show that the figure of 334 men or 41% exaggerates the representation of business in this parliament, and that the number of those whose major incomes derived from or whose major efforts went into business was in all probability substantially less.

For further light on the problem of social differentiation and for a partial answer to the second of the questions listed on pages 250–251 we may now examine, as this method enables us to do, the extent to which men with various kinds of social position went into various kinds of economic enterprises. Let us take first the simplest and crudest figures, and pass on later to the refinements. We may begin by taking as a unit the total group of all those belonging to or related by male descent to the peerage, baronetage and landed gentry. This group, to save space, may be summarily abbrevi-

ated to "PBG," and those not in it may be described as "non-PBG." The PBG, it will be remembered, amounted to 71% of the membership of parliament and the non-PBG to 29%. A cross-check of these figures with the figures on business interests shows that the PBG as a whole tended in proportion to their numbers to enter business decidedly less than did the non-PBG. Only 35% of the PBG were in business of any kind, while the proportion of the non-PBG in business was 56% or just over half.

A more detailed break-down brings out features which the general figures do not reveal. Certain social groups, the relatives of peers, the heirs to baronetcies, and the heirs to landed estates, went very little into business of any kind, except for becoming railway directors, which was apparently a line of activity that attracted everybody. Furthermore, some of the PBG entered businesses that were not time-consuming: they became, for example, directors of railways or insurance companies, where their role was possibly more one of ornament than of utility. The advantage of getting a title on a board of directors is proverbial. Members of the PBG were somewhat less active in commerce and manufacture. One can arrange the different types of business in a rough scale according to the social connections of those engaging in them. The only types of businesses where the PBG decidedly outnumbered the non-PBG were mines and railways. Among merchants and manufacturers, the non-PBG, despite their relatively small representation in this parliament, outnumbered the PBG 2 to 1. In most other businesses the PBG and the non-PBG were about evenly balanced.

These figures suggest that there is a limited case, a certain amount of evidence, for the theory that there existed among the members of this parliament a dichotomy between land and business. Yet this is only a part of the story, and surely the most striking feature of the figures is the amount of overlapping they reveal between those with social position and those engaged in business enterprise. Doubtless this is partly due to the fact that some of the economic interests listed, such as mining, canals, docks or railways, may be and in many of these cases probably were directly connected with the exploitation of the resources of landed estates. The possession of land may lead a man into business by any of several different paths, and in cases such as these the distinction between land and business is particularly artificial. Yet the business ventures of the PBG were by no means limited to enterprises of this type.

There is not space now for further nuances, but from the figures as a whole it is evident that it is impossible to set up any clear general distinction between the nobility and gentry on the one hand and those engaged in business on the other. The cases of overlapping are numerous enough to invalidate altogether so simple a line of division. To make a formal differentiation between land and business or between aristocracy and middle class is to freeze unjustifiably a contemporary rule of thumb. Indeed, throughout the detailed research I have constantly been impressed by the comparative homogeneity of this parliament by any of the ordinary standards of social measurement. These men were for the most part wealthy, persons of consequence in their own communities, an *élite* who in their general character and composition differed profoundly from the population of England as a whole.

In assigning party labels this study has followed the terminology of Dod's *Parliamentary Companion* for the 1840's, the only major addition being that those Conservatives who voted for Corn Law repeal in the third reading of the Corn Law bill in 1846 have been occasionally referred to as "Peelites." No detailed account of parties can be attempted here, but three points of special interest emerged from the tabulations which may supply at least a partial answer to the third of the general questions raised at the beginning.

In the first place there appeared a general line of differentiation between the Conservatives as a whole and the Whigs, Liberals and Reformers as a whole. Of these two general groups, the Conservatives tended more to be related to the peerage, baronetage and gentry, they tended less to have a business interest, they were slightly younger, and a larger proportion of them had attended public school and university.

The second point of interest is the extent of the similarity between the two kinds of Conservatives. One would conjecture that the Peelites might differ from other Conservatives in their social and economic circumstances in a way that would foreshadow their eventual break with the party. The results do not confirm this expectation. In social composition the two groups are very similar. In economic interest they differ, the Peelites tending to have proportionately more business interests. However, these are largely of a minor or incidental character, and in the amount of major business interests Peelites and other Conservatives are almost exactly alike.

In the third place, and this is perhaps the most important point, the men with business interests in this parliament divided themselves almost equally between the Conservative group and the general group composed of Whigs, Liberals and Reformers. Although the group of Liberal parties was smaller, and hence the representation of business in it proportionately greater, the fact remains that a businessman in this parliament was almost as likely to be a Conservative as he was to be on the other side. This even split continues for the most part in the break-down by individual businesses, the principal exceptions being that East India proprietors, metal manufacturers and colliery owners tended to the Conservative side, while those in other types of manufacture, commerce and finance tended to the Liberal side. Bankers, railway directors, those engaged in other types of mining, and most of the other groups divided almost evenly.

The "ten hours" issue[1] does not bulk large in the total work of this parliament. It is nevertheless of considerable historical

[1] See note on p. 47.

interest and makes a convenient and manageable question to select as an illustration of the relation of biographical data to voting behaviour. On this issue there are four usable divisions in 1844 and four in 1847 (as well as one in 1846 which there is not space to discuss). By taking account of the votes in all four divisions in each year it has been possible to get the attitudes of a considerable number of men. The very few cases of inconsistent voting in either year as well as the much larger number of abstentions have been omitted from this simplified statement.

With votes, as with biographical information, it is necessary to allow for a margin of error. There are obvious misprints in Hansard, which leads to the inference that there may be other misprints which are not obvious. Pairs of men with the same or similar names create problems of identity that are sometimes insoluble. Beyond this, some votes were undoubtedly cast by mistake and do not correctly indicate the opinion of the voter. On one occasion Sir George De Lacy Evans was by accident locked in the house when the Ayes were sent forth and he was numbered against his intention among the Noes. One cannot help wondering how often this sort of thing happened without the fact being recorded. Yet on the whole these difficulties do not appear great, and it seems reasonable to believe that figures on votes can be used with somewhat more confidence than figures on biographical data.

With regard to party vote on the "ten hours" question, a matter relating to the fourth of the general issues raised on a previous page, it seems to take as a starting-point what has become almost the standard interpretation. This is that, while some Whigs and Liberals were late and reluctant converts to the cause, the "ten hours" measure was initiated and principally supported by the Conservatives or by a Tory-Radical alliance. A study of the detailed figures suggests some qualifications of this view:

1. The Conservatives, though they strongly supported the measure in 1847, were not its supporters from the beginning. On the contrary, when it came up in 1844 they actually opposed it by a small but clear majority. This, I believe, has not been pointed out before. Thus the overwhelming Protectionist support for "ten hours" in 1847, far from being grounded on a basic and unchanging Conservative philosophy or mode of action, was a sudden conversion.

2. The Whigs and Liberals did not originally oppose the measure but, on the contrary, when it was brought up in 1844, were its strongest supporters.

3. The passing of the "ten hours" bill in 1847 was not due to the conversion of the Whigs, as in the old interpretation, but to the conversion of the Protectionists. Whigs and Liberals tended to support the cause in 1844 and so far as they moved in the intervening three years they moved against it, being almost equally divided on it in 1847.

4. Nor was the "ten hours" cause supported by a Tory-Radical alliance. In fact for the year 1844, before party politics were clouded by the Conservative split on the Corn Law question, this statement is almost the exact opposite of the truth: in 1844 both Conservatives and Reformers opposed the measure by very slight majorities, while Whigs and Liberals supported it by proportionately larger majorities. In 1847 the Conservatives had swung round, but the Reformers were still almost evenly divided.

Unfortunately there is not space to discuss at length the implications of these figures or the hypotheses that might account for them. It is necessary to pass on to the last of the questions raised at the beginning of this paper, the relation of social and economic data to votes.

Consider first the two general groups of PBG and non-PBG. In 1844 the PBG slightly supported "ten hours" and the non-PBG slightly opposed it. But the majorities in each case were insignificant and in view of the margin of error for which allowance must always be made it seems proper to describe both groups as being about evenly divided on the issue in 1844. In 1847 each group favoured the measure in approximately the same proportion, about 2 to 1.

The inference from these figures, if correct, is sensational enough: it is that social position had almost no statistical relation to votes on the "ten hours" issue. This result is so contrary to the whole tradition of our thinking on the question that the obvious next step is to turn to a detailed break-down of social position for further information. Yet even the break-down reveals few important differences in any single group, except for categories where the figures are too small to support a heavy superstructure of deductions. While these figures should be treated with caution, and there is further work to be done on them, yet so far as they go they seem to make serious inroads on the theory of aristocratic benevolence.

It is a tempting hypothesis that votes, if they do not relate to social position, may relate to the supposedly more basic fact of economic interest. The figures appear to give some but not decisive support to this view. In both 1844 and 1847 non-business elements were somewhat more friendly to "ten hours" than were business elements. Yet the exceptions are numerous enough to show that a simple and general explanation of this sort is by no means adequate.

The break-down of economic interests provides some surprises. We might expect the principal opponents of the bill to be the manufacturers; these, however, were for it by a clear majority both in 1844 and 1847. On the other hand the greatest opposition in both years came from the merchants who were joined in 1844, curiously enough, by the East India proprietors. Yet on the whole the detailed figures add little. For most of the individual business interests the prevailing pattern both in 1844 and in 1847 was a substantial group on each side of the issue.

Two conclusions appear warranted: 1. Having a business interest does have some statistical relation to the "ten hours" vote, since those with business interests tended to be somewhat less favourable to the cause than those without them. 2. On the other hand having a business interest, whether "active" or incidental, did not apparently decide the issue. Both as a whole and individually the different business groups tended to split on it. Hence economic interest, as an explanation of votes on the "ten hours" question, seems of little use.

The foregoing statements are by no means final and are designed merely to illustrate the possibilities of a method. Much further study is needed before any of these questions can be answered with certainty or completeness. Perhaps enough has been said, however, to indicate how these techniques can be used to cast light on such intricate and difficult problems as the social composition of parliament, the overlapping of different social and economic groups, and the relation of party, social position and economic interest to voting behaviour.

The burden of these remarks has been negative. I have tried to suggest that some previously held opinions may have to be considerably qualified, and have made adverse comments, so far as the very limited evidence permitted, on such large general theories as aristocratic benevolence, Tory paternalism, and economic determinism. On the other hand I have not brought forward any new large general theory to take their place. This negative approach seems altogether reasonable and appropriate. In an age so complex and confused as that of early Victorian England one does not immediately arrive at simple and complete explanations. In the present state of knowledge it may be more to the point to reach a basis of fact which compels us to look critically at the intellectual framework in which we have been accustomed to discuss this period, to jettison catch-phrases, and to appreciate more deeply the difficulties of generalization.

The Agricultural Interest and Corn Law Repeal

G. KITSON CLARK

G. Kitson Clark (born 1900), former fellow of Trinity College and Reader in Constitutional History at Cambridge University, has written articles on the British electorate and the repeal of the Corn Laws as well as two fine books, *Peel and the Conservative Party* (1929) and *The Making of Victorian England* (1962) (the Ford Lectures of 1960). He notes that after 1832, the aristocracy maintained its social and political power. His interpretation of the repeal of the Corn Laws stresses less the conflict between economic and social groups than the political motivation of the aristocracy. He suggests that the aristocracy was willing to repeal the Corn Laws to maintain political power. This conclusion coincides with that of many analysts of the reform bill, including G. Macaulay Trevelyan, who emphasize the concession theory, the view that the bill was passed to keep the aristocracy in political power.

THE INFLUENCE of economic interests on the play of party politics has long been realized to be a subject well worthy of study: as worthy of study, though perhaps less often studied, is the influence of party politics, or of party feelings and the social preferences and animosities that invigorate them, on men's thoughts about their economic interest: and so perhaps on economic theory. It is in order to raise these issues that I wish to return to the old history of the struggle that culminated in the repeal of the Corn Laws in 1846. . . .

It may help to throw light on the subject if the attack on the Corn Laws is considered for a moment not as a clear demonstration of economic truth, not even as a dispassionate statement of economic opinion, but more as an outpouring of social emotion, using a symbol or a myth as a catalyst. There is perhaps some excuse for this view in the fact that the attack was launched so fiercely on this particular point by these particular men at this moment. Let us grant that their opinions were directed by all the tendencies then fashionable in economic thought; let us also grant,

as we must, that it was natural for them to believe that the Corn Laws enhanced the price of bread to the poor and to be angry about it: yet it may not be unjust to suggest that Manchester manufacturers were as much moved by the depression in British industry as by the price of bread, even if it were the bread of the poor. But here the connexion with the Corn Laws was less obvious. After all, between 1815 and 1837, in spite of the Corn Laws, British industry and the British export trade had enjoyed their most extraordinary development. Nor, quite patently, had the slump been caused by the Corn Laws. It had been caused by the classical causes of slumps; overproduction, over-speculation and a financial breakdown in the United States. The distress which the leaguers made the burden of so much of their oratory was, again obviously, largely caused by the slump, and had the same origins.

Nevertheless, to these men, able and sincere as they were, all hell was caused by the Corn Laws and all heaven was to be won by their repeal. About the way in which that heaven was to be won they

From G. Kitson Clark, "The Repeal of the Corn Laws and the Politics of the Forties," *Economic History Review*, 2d Series, IV (1951), pp. 1, 3–13. Reprinted by permission of the author and the *Economic History Review*.

were not consistent, or rather their opinions developed, and altered, as the demands of controversy developed. Certainly within two or three years they seem to have changed their minds on the probable effect of repeal on labour costs, on the price of bread, on the prosperity of the farmer and even upon rents. Of course, Cobden produced the best line of argument in pressing the idea that if we took more corn from abroad foreigners would take more of our goods, and the history of our trade with the Levant in the years immediately after repeal seems to support his contention. But did not Cobden himself, in the heat of controversy, exaggerate the general importance of this? Certainly it seems doubtful how valid his argument was when applied, as he frequently applied it, to the United States which had not at that moment much corn to send us, but from whom we were normally taking greedily as much raw cotton as we could lay our hands on.

Perhaps then this angry exaggerated concentration on one single partially irrelevant factor suggests that these men's opinions were informed at least as much by passion as by science. And is that unusual in economic controversies that are also political? In these matters are not men's psychological needs apt to come first and their arguments and explanations later to endorse conclusions already commended by their emotions? And when they consider their troubles, do not men most normally need two things, an elixir to promise salvation and a scape-goat on which to lay the blame? But the scape-goat must be human. It is well, of course, to label the cause of all troubles with some large-sounding abstraction like protection, capitalism, socialism, communism; but that will not really satisfy unless men can feel that behind that label lurks somebody making evil profit out of their misfortunes. And it will be best of all if men can discover, without surprise, that the whole world is suffering from evils which have been caused by the wickedness of exactly the kind of persons they most dislike.

But to explain why this was true of the manufacturers and the Corn Laws, it is necessary to turn to the structure of the England of the early nineteenth century. In that England there were two societies living cheek by jowl. On the one hand, there was a new self-confident society: the men who were making fortunes and changing the world by means of the new industrial methods, and behind them a mass of others, substantial tradesmen, dissenting shopkeepers and what used to be called intelligent artisans. Alongside of these, and detested by them, was a much older aristocratic England, the England of noblemen, squires and parsons who dominated, and so it seemed to their enemies, exploited for their own selfish benefit all the institutions of the country. Indeed, to fill in the picture there might be said to be a third and more unhappy England, the second nation of Disraeli's novel *Sybil*, the nation of the poor, in whose interests each side in this controversy continually, and not insincerely, claimed to speak. But probably, if any generalization can be hazarded, neither side had the confidence of this other nation; nor with such spectres as those of the worst-situated farm labourers, or of the hand-loom weavers, or of the factory children in the background, did either side deserve it.

But for our purposes the effective nation can be divided into those two great societies which we can call very loosely the aristocracy and the great middle class. The boundaries were not clearly defined. Some of the most important men engaged in the older commercial activities like shipping and banking were Tory, and in towns such as Leeds, Sunderland, Bristol, Liverpool, there was a Tory nucleus, while some of the new railway interest was Tory, as was King Hudson himself. On the other hand, certain Whigs or Liberals, though born members of the older society, worked in close alliance with the League. Indeed the line which best marks the division between the two societies is not economic or political, but religious, the line between the Church of England and Protestant Dissent.

It is necessary to read contemporary literature to realize the full violence of the Dissenting attacks on the Church of England at this time. It is more than theological; it is pregnant with the festering bitterness of one class at another whom they believe to be insolently privileged at their expense. The attack on the Corn Laws was in the same vein, for the laws were held to protect the unjust advantages of the insolent nobility, of the fat Church of England bishops and rectors and of the booby squires. It was, as Bright said, "a movement of the commercial and industrious classes against the lords and great proprietors of the soil."

In such circumstances, it was perhaps natural that Cobden should see the advantage of infusing as he said "a moral and even a religious spirit into the topic." Moreover, he realized that the most successful middle-class agitation so far had been religious, the anti-slavery agitation. So he obtained the services of Joseph Sturge and George Thompson, the hero of a famous crusade in the United States in the cause of the abolitionists, and Thompson organized on his behalf a meeting of nearly 700 ministers of religion in Manchester whom Cobden asked to declare that the Corn Laws were "opposed to the law of God . . . anti-scriptural and anti-religious." Needless to say he gained the necessary anathemas, and in that sign they went forward to conquer, so that ever afterwards the cause of free trade in this country has had a curious holy smell about it which the actual subject-matter of the theory would not seem to warrant.

And what of the fortress they were to attack? It was ancient, grotesque and formidable. The old aristocratic society of England may have had many of the vices peculiar to an aristocracy; but one vice it did lack, it was not decadent. The business of war, the business of sport, the business of agriculture and the business of politics all brought its members into the outer world into positions which they may not have deserved, but in which they had to show ability, enterprise, nerve, or, at the lowest, animal courage. For instance, there is every reason to think that the Earl of Cardigan was no suitable commander for the Light Brigade of Cavalry at the Battle of Balaclava, but at least he did ride the regulation five horses' lengths in front of his men right up to the Russian batteries, while the career of the Duke of Wellington is not the only reminder that this class could throw up very much greater captains in war than the Earl of Cardigan. Sport is traditionally own cousin to war and in such matters as hunting and racing the nobility and gentry presided over a very rough world indeed. Here again they might gain their positions by right of their broad acres or great wealth, but they had to retain them by bodily prowess or sometimes by physical strength. In Squire Osbaldestone's autobiography you will find it on record how he had to fight a much larger man with his bare fists or charge a very angry crowd armed only with a light hunting crop to keep due order in the hunting field or on the racecourse. Perhaps, however, more to our purpose is the force of character by which Lord George Bentinck imposed his own standards on the racing world, and the infernal dogged obstinacy with which he insisted in 1835 on going out to fight a duel with Squire Osbaldestone who had, in his view, broken the ethics of racing at his expense. It was apparently going to certain death, since the Squire had once for a bet placed ten pistol shots on the ace of diamonds at twenty yards, and Lord George was not a particularly good shot.

The basis of this society was agricultural, and here it is germane to remember that the very remarkable revolution that was going forward in British agriculture in the nineteenth century was the work not only of practical farmers and scientists, but also of squires and noblemen. Coke of Norfolk, Philip Pusey, Sir John Bennet Lawes, the fifth Duke of Bedford, the third Earl Spencer and others created a very considerable legacy not only for Britain, but for the world. But the most absorbing occupation was politics. The nobility and their relations and nominees filled courts and cabinets and, with the squires, occupied a wholly disproportionate section of the House of Commons. Again there was in the background a very rough world, as can be seen from the many accounts of the innumerable disputed elections over which they expended so much energy and money. Indeed many things in life can have been more agreeable than trying to address from the hustings a mob which at the same time was by tradition trying its skill at a relatively easy mark with spittle, dirt, dead animals or, in Kent, old pieces of bullock's liver flicked from the end of a stick, which were a local specialty.

Of course in that world they were very strongly entrenched. The British House of Commons had been reformed in 1832, but in truth the eighteenth century still stalked many of the constituencies of Great Britain and Ireland, if not quite naked, still as ever unashamed. In many cases it was still blandly accepted as a rule that a man's tenants, dependants and employees should vote as he directed; such influence as attached to the various persons of importance in a constituency went to make up what was called, in the jargon of the day, the "interest" in it. In many constituencies the "interest" was divided, and these were the scenes of traditional battles between two families or groups of families, in some no effective "interest" existed, and in certain constituencies one "interest" was overwhelming or at least good for one seat. For instance, it is stated in Dod's *Electoral Facts,* published in 1852, that in Tavistock, the influence "possessed by the Duke of Bedford is paramount; his friends and relatives have never been rejected." In Peterborough, the influence is "wholly in the hands of the Earl of FitzWilliam." Of Chester and the Marquis of Westminster it is said that "with trifling exceptions some member of his family has sat since the restoration," and of the Wick district in Scotland the influence "possessed by the Duke of Sutherland is paramount here; the

auditor of his Graces' estates has sat for twenty-two years."

Moreover, the distribution of seats grossly favoured the aristocracy and it grossly favoured agriculture. Out of a house of 658 members the English counties produced no less than 144, and, in addition, there were 15 county members for Wales, 30 for Scotland, 64 for Ireland. Many small country towns enjoyed equal representation with some of the largest cities in the land. Thus Thetford, in the wilds of Norfolk, with about 200 electors and a population of about 4000 returned two members to Parliament which was the same number as Manchester; Malton, in Yorkshire, two members, which was the same as Birmingham. The boroughs of Dorset, Devonshire and Wiltshire produced 34 members and their whole population was certainly less than Liverpool with again only two representatives. And behind the House of Commons frowned the battlements of the House of Lords.

Yet in eight years the Corn Laws were repealed, after only one general election conducted in circumstances unfavourable to the League. Now why was this? Of course part of the answer is Peel's conversion. But that is only part of the answer; it is still necessary to explain how Peel was able to complete his task, and to explain not only Peel's conversion itself but also Lord John Russell's conversion and indeed the conversion of almost everyone of Cabinet rank in either party all at about the same time.

And in order to reach a satisfactory explanation it is necessary to make a distinction which historians have normally failed to make, and which Cobden and Bright did not want to make; the distinction between those elements which were primarily aristocratic and political and those which were primarily agricultural. The point is suggested by an analysis of the third reading in May, 1846, of Peel's Corn Importation Bill. On that division 327 voted in favour and 229 against. The group of constituencies producing the largest number of votes against the bill and 25 in its favour to be compared, for instance, to the English Boroughs with 210 votes for the bill and 82 against. Now the county constituency is often represented as being entirely under the control of the landowners and nobility. Certainly to represent the county was a highly estimated honour; the county member ranked only behind such men as the Lord-Lieutenant, the Master of Foxhounds and the Chairman of Quarter Sessions in the estimation of county society, and a man's tenants were normally expected to help him, or someone he favoured, to gain the position.

But that did not mean that a county member could vote as he pleased. Even the landlord-tenant relationship was by no means a one-way relationship. Probably if he wanted to work his estate, a landlord had to respect the opinions of his farming tenants; certainly in many cases he thought it his duty to do so. For instance, when the Duke of Rutland heard what Peel intended to do in 1846, he was at a loss how he ought to vote in the House of Lords, so he rode round the tenants and labourers on his estate to ask their opinion, and it was apparently what the labourers told him that decided him to vote against the measure. This was perhaps not typical, but there exists a good deal of evidence that farming opinion, tenant or freehold, counted for a good deal in county elections and was rather anxiously considered by county members whenever agricultural matters were to the fore. Indeed there appears to be evidence that various country gentlemen were pushed in 1846 into a rather unwilling opposition to repeal from behind by the farmers.

All this fits in with a recent article on the protectionist agitations in 1844–6. The author, Mr. Mosse of the State University, Iowa, pointed out that the main force of those agitations came from the tenant farmers, and indeed that their violence and their attacks on the leaders of the Conservative party were much disliked by the county magnates. But Mr. Mosse did not push his inquiries far enough back. These agitations had been going on for some time among the farmers and some of the country gentry certainly since 1834, probably since 1815. The subject-matter was not always the Corn Laws. The deflationary return to a currency based on gold in 1819 has been a bitter source of grievance, so was the tax on malt, but the same personalities were normally involved and the shape of the agitation was always the same, many farmers and some country gentlemen against the government of the day and also against the leaders of the Tory party when a Whig government was in power.

In fact, the position was this. Agriculture as an industry, the largest industry in the country, was going through very hard times. In its agony it appealed to government to help it out, and it gained one concession, the Corn Law of 1815, but that Law never produced the security that was promised and was constantly modified to the disadvantage of the farmer. In the matter of the return to cash payments, which was probably much nearer to the real source of their trouble, and in the matter of taxation, those who claimed to speak for the landed interest could never get the concessions they wanted. Therefore it is not surprising that the final repeal of the Corn Laws in 1846 was in their view only the culmination of a series of desertions and betrayals, in many of which Sir Robert Peel had been the main figure. He had been mainly responsible for the currency act in 1819, and in his ministry of 1834–5 his one victory had been to resist a determined attempt to repeal the malt tax.

But Peel was not the only Tory statesman to fail the land in this way. Even in the unreformed 1820's Lord Liverpool can be found disappointing the agriculturists, and Lord Castlereagh begging the radical Ricardo to teach his agricultural followers a little economics. Nor is the explanation of this diversionism far to seek. However important an industry and however powerful its political position, a statesman in charge of the whole country must take into account the needs of other interests unless he is politically stupid or morally irresponsible, and the men who normally governed Great Britain were neither. But this means that your statesmen will always disappoint the representatives of a single interest, for he will always see more than the other and see differently. The view from the windows of Downing Street will always be more extensive and varied that what a man sees angrily from his own stackyard or the parlour of his country house; and as a man sees, so will he act.

More than this, no statesman can work in isolation, few statesmen can extemporize economic doctrine, and it is probably better that they should not try to do so. A statesman therefore must work in accord with the assumptions of the dominant economic thought of the day. Indeed it may well be that in many periods on many subjects, there will, in reality, be only one policy for any government to follow, one policy which satisfies the conjunction of the contemporary climate of opinion, the views of available experts and civil servants and the needs of the moment, and that a great deal of the business of party politicians is to pretend that there will be differences where no differences can be. Certainly, in the first half of the nineteenth century there was only one road along which a major British statesman could travel, the road that led by Political Economy to Free Trade. A population that had doubled itself and would double itself again, an export trade that stretched forth its hands triumphantly into the four quarters of the globe, and the interpretative work of the great classical economists — all these spelt one thing, free trade, and to that bourne they all came in the end.

It is true that the doctrine that we must buy in the cheapest and sell in the dearest market might seem likely to be hard on negative agriculture, and Peel was by no means the only man to linger a little over protection to corn as an exception to other rules. But the necessities of the period led him forward, and it was easy to be convinced that those very necessities would also provide a solution to this problem of agriculture. Surely, it could be argued, a rapidly increasing population, particularly if it enjoyed the prosperity free trade would give it, would maintain a continuous demand for the home producer to satisfy, and the corn and meat grown at home would in general almost always supply most of that market most cheaply. Of course the British farmer would be better able to play his part and pay his way if he took advantage of the remarkable improvements in agricultural technique in the development of which so many of the peerage and larger landed gentry were engaged. But surely with the application to the land of capital, which Peel in 1846 took some steps to supply, and of science, which Peel said in 1846 was only in its infancy, British agriculture need fear nothing.

Certainly those arguments seemed reasonable enough to great nobles whose rent roles were comfortably supplemented by revenue from mines, or docks, or urban property. They even satisfied those whose sources of revenue were primarily agricultural, but whose estates had provided a surplus which could be used to tide over bad times or to use the new technique of deep drainage or the other facilities that were now offering themselves. They did not console farmers who thought that they might be ruined by one year's drop in price, who had perhaps little capital and no science; or who at least would not trust science as the panacea to the troubles from which they knew they were suffering, like the farmers who opposed even the foundation of the Royal Agricultural Society in 1839 as "delusive in principle" because its constitution precluded agitating the cause of protection. Just as political influence descended by the usual channels from the party leaders, so agricultural opinion worked its way upwards from the level of the farmers. It influenced those country gentlemen who spent most of their lives immersed in the life of the county, it influenced the county members whose constituents the farmers were, it influenced those great magnates like the Duke of Richmond who valued their position as leaders of the agricultural community more highly than anything that politics could give, and it caused strange difficulties in the breast of a man like the Duke of Buckingham who wanted to be both the "farmer's friend" and to enjoy those prizes, the garter, a Lord Lieutenancy, a variety of jobs for dependants, which Peel had in his pocket for magnates who behaved well; while certain of the more foolish country magnates like that tragic old goose, the Duke of Newcastle, or the Duke of Buckingham again who had bought land on so extravagant a scale to keep up their position that they too had probably too little liquid capital to improve their estates or even to work them properly. Probably they, too, could not view an unprotected future with any degree of confidence.

Of course the belief in the necessity of the Corn Laws was as much emotionally conceived as the contrary opinion was in the breasts of the leaguers, particularly after the League had raised the temperature of the question. Surtees, the novelist, says of the farmers of Durham that they did not clearly know what would happen if the Corn Laws were repealed, but that they were sure it would be something very dreadful. To many farmers, and to not a few landowners, the Corn Laws also became a myth or a symbol, and the statistics they used had obviously been collected to prove an already firm conviction. Not that the arguments which were put forward on their behalf were as contemptible as they are usually said to have been. In fact some of the "heresies" and "fallacies" put forward by protectionists would seem to need but a little redressing to be turned into statements about the importance of full employment and the value of a managed currency to pass muster as the orthodoxies of modern economic controversy.

But that does not matter at all; their thought was in the wrong phase and what they said was treated with contempt, and

ruled out of court. The country party had probably always been weaker than the political interests that ruled Britain. In fact, the crisis of 1846 showed how weak they were. Never was there an occasion on which the landed interest had better chance of success. The suddenness of Peel's conversion, and the great violence of the League, had shocked many people into opposition to Peel who would otherwise have followed their natural leaders. The Parliament of 1846 was a Tory Parliament, and on this occasion the landed interest had what they normally lacked, able leadership and debating power. The tongue of Benjamin Disraeli had a sharper cutting edge than that of the ordinary puzzle-headed country gentleman, and Lord George Bentinck felt about Peel's conduct as he had felt about the Squire's lapse in 1835 or the gang who had faked "Running Rein" in the Derby of 1844; therefore with raucous voice, a knowledge of statistics that stank of the midnight oil, but with considerable ability and unwavering vindictiveness, he hunted Peel down.

Certainly the country party made a better showing than Peel expected. He believed from experience he could manage them, indeed two years before he had told his intimates that people "like being governed," a disputable proposition. But the debates on this measure were prolonged *ad nauseam*; more country gentlemen, the kind of men Bagehot called "the finest brute votes in Europe," spoke than probably had ever spoken before; the Tory party was broken in two, and Peel driven from office. But none of this could save the Corn Laws. The apparatus of political control and influence by which the country was normally governed was turned against them. Bentinck complained of the number of placemen voting for Peel. For other purposes I once worked out a list of boroughs in which it was possible that government influence was either considerable or predominating and I found it produced 21 votes for the repeal of the Corn Laws and 2 against. I have already mentioned a number of boroughs where aristocratic influence predominated. The votes from every one of these boroughs were cast in favour of repeal. It is true that there were other pocket boroughs on the other side, but the list of all boroughs in England with less than 500 constituents, those tiny boroughs of whom John Bright said later that "for the most part they cannot pretend to the power of free election in any way whatsoever" produced 34 votes against the repeal and 50 in its favour, or in the United Kingdom 37 and 68; while a fair proportion of these counties whose members voted for repeal were notoriously under the control of some predominating aristocratic influence.

Of course, much of this influence was Whig. The Tories were too much shattered by Peel's sudden change to produce more than 108 votes in the final division, but considering the past of the Whigs, considering how much of their power was based on the large landowners, considering the fact that their leader had only been converted to total repeal in the previous autumn, it is a remarkable tribute to their party loyalty and discipline that in the final result only nine Whigs voted against the repeal, five of whom were county members. And the passage of the measure through the House of Lords probably demonstrates the military discipline which the Duke of Wellington enforced on that body for its own good.

But can all this be called in any simple sense the "victory of the Middle Class"? Of course their part had been important, and the nationalist Irish also had provided votes for repeal, but would it not be equally correct to call it "a concession by the aristocracy," a timely retreat, that is, from a forward position that had proved to be dangerous? If so, they had their reward. After the battle the power remained in the same kind of hands as those in which it had rested before. It is true that the governments of the period that followed were nominally Whig, but it was men like Lord Palmerston and Lord John Russell who continued to direct policy and form governments, not men like Cobden and Bright.

If behind the demand for the repeal there had lurked other middle-class aspirations, they were frustrated. In 1848, Bright, naturally in confident mood, expressed the belief that they would soon proceed to a real reform of the elective system of the country which he said was a "sham" disguising the control of the country by the titled and proprietary classes. He was the more deceived. The next reform Bill was not till 1867, and vote by ballot not till 1872. Other movements had been set on foot about this time; the complete suffrage movement, the anti-state church movement. They were all without effect. Complete suffrage had to wait, the Church of England was never disestablished, even the House of Lords retained its powers intact till after the end of the century. No doubt this was partly due to the anodyne of prosperity and partly to a relaxation of emotional and intellectual tension, which for various reasons took place in the middle of the nineteenth century. But may it not also have been due to the loss of that emotive symbol, the bread tax, which had united so much force behind the Anti-Corn Law League?

In fact, saving common sense had again saved the British upper-classes. No doubt the British middle classes were powerful in mid-Victorian Britain, but that period might also be called the Indian summer of the British aristocracy, as also it is in many ways the golden age of British farming. That continuation of aristocratic rule was not only part of Peel's achievement, it had also been one of his objects. On the third reading of the Corn Importation Bill he said "Sir, if I look to the prerogatives of the crown, if I look to the position of the Church, if I look to the influence of the aristocracy, I cannot charge myself with having taken any course inconsistent with Conservative principles."

His claim was well justified, in fact he could go further; he could claim that he had saved the aristocracy by enabling it to side step from the blow which the organized passion of the Anti-Corn Law movement had threatened to deliver. But he could not have done that if the passions, or opinions, or interests of the great aristocracy, or of those who really governed the country had really been hopelessly committed to the other side.

IV. A CONSERVATIVE REVISION

The Other Face of Reform — A Conservative View

D. C. MOORE

D. C. Moore (1925–   ) studied at Columbia and Cambridge universities where he was a student of G. Kitson Clark. He has taught at Harpur College and the University of California, Los Angeles. In a significant article, "The Other Face of Reform," *Victorian Studies*, V (1961–1962), Moore rejects the concession theory of the first reform bill. He points out that in Britain, political democracy was established by parliamentary vote rather than by revolution and each reform of parliament was carried by an unreformed parliament. His investigation of the external agitation for reform reveals that the bill was supported by an urban-rural coalition. In two other articles, "Concession or Cure: The Sociological Premises of the First Reform Act," *The Historical Journal*, IX (1966) and "Social Structure, Political Structure, and Public Opinion in Mid-Victorian England," R. Robson, ed., *Ideas and Institutions of the Victorians* (Cambridge, 1967), Moore amplifies and clarifies the arguments suggested in "The Other Face of Reform."

I N MOST OF nineteenth-century Europe the growth of political democracy was essentially revolutionary. It has therefore been understood in terms of the class antagonisms which are said to have caused the Continental revolutions. In Britain, on the other hand, political democracy was established by parliamentary vote, not by revolution, by deliberation among members of the established ruling classes, not by decree of popular tribunal. The British experience would therefore seem to require a separate interpretative framework. This historians have not provided. While in England Reform Acts take the place of revolution, they are fitted to the general revolutionary pattern.

The equation of reform and revolution has held the field since the early nineteenth century. It is not unreasonable. It derives from much contemporary evidence and involves well-established social theory. Obviously, reform can not be isolated from the general context of economic and social change. Obviously, too, before the cycles of reform began, many members of the industrial middle classes were deeply annoyed at the lack of correspondence between their increasing economic strength and their continuing representational weakness in Parliament. Again, the passage of each of the three major Reform Acts was attended with considerable public disorder. And still again, following each Act the newly enfranchised classes were the beneficiaries of considerable legislative attention. In these circumstances, historians have tended to introduce the protagonists of reform almost solely against the background of increasing industrialization; they have tended to attribute the occurrence of reform almost solely to the activities of the various industrial classes, or to men who are regarded as their advocates; they have tended to find

From D. C. Moore, "The Other Face of Reform," *Victorian Studies*, V (1961–1962), pp. 7–13, 17–34. Reprinted by permission of the author and *Victorian Studies*.

the meaning of reform almost solely in the needs of these new classes. Considering that each successive Reform Act was passed by an unreformed Parliament this view of the total process carries its own interpretational imperative — that each Act was a concession by which the established ruling classes managed to prevent the outbreak of revolution.

Yet for several reasons, if we take the first Reform Act as an example, this concession theory is not altogether satisfactory. In the first place, it prematurely sets the stage for an urban middle-class drama. As recent studies have increasingly tended to show, the first Reform Act did not mark a clear break in English political life. Least of all did it mark the arrival of the urban middle class to political life. Least of all did it mark the arrival of the urban middle class to political power. In the second place, it tends to assume an unwarranted modernity in early nineteenth-century electoral behavior. And finally, it tends to distort the reform calendar.

The standard chronology of the first Reform Act posits two essential penultimate events, the death of George IV and the July Revolution in Paris. The latter bears the burden of reawakening reformist sentiments which had lain dormant for many years, the former of transmitting these sentiments to Parliament. Because George's death required that elections take place within six months it is used as the occasion when many persons, inspired by the example of Paris, entered Parliament. However, as Professor Gash has shown, many English elections were already well under way before news of the Revolution arrived. Indeed, reform emerged from its hibernation not in the summer of 1830 but a year earlier. In the summer of 1829 it appealed neither to the aristocratic Whigs nor the urban Liberals. Apart from the Radicals, its perennial advocates, reform appealed to many Ultra-Tories, or, to use a more generic term, to many members of the Country Party. It showed the extent of their hostility towards Wellington.

It is true that the demand for political reform had long been associated with the Foxite Whigs, Liberals, and Radicals. Yet in the immediate pre-reform years it was largely monopolized by the Country Party. While it may be an exaggeration to designate as a Party the heterogeneous group of active opponents to Wellington's Government in 1829 and 1830, their opposition, as well as their demands for political, fiscal, and tariff reforms, were major phenomena of these years and important factors in the elections of 1830. As will be seen, however, by the spring of 1831 the exigencies of parliamentary politics tended to induce an historical amnesia. The efforts of the administrative Tories to reconstitute a Party after their defeat the previous November were hardly compatible with the memory that numerous Tories had played major roles in defeating them. Furthermore, because the possibility of Country Party parentage could lead to expectations that the reform progeny would take after its parents by showing a tendency towards inflation or a renewal of protection, Liberals, Radicals, and many Whigs found it essential to deny this possibility outright and to claim the baby for their own. Their plea, which the administrative Tories did their best to support, was contained in two assertions: first, that reform was a Whig-Liberal-Radical monopoly, and second, that the issue of reform was fundamentally social.

Because these assertions won the day, most historians have ignored the Country Party's demands for reform, or, like Halévy, have deprecated them on two grounds: that they "lacked the support of the Whig or Liberal party leaders," and that they "lacked the support of the masses." The first of these arguments is tied to the notion that the Reform Ministry was a Whig Ministry, a notion which Professor Aspinall has recently tried to correct. The other is tied to the notion that the course of history in both the long and short term is defined by popular desires. While it must be allowed that this latter notion has some pertinence today, when means for transforming such desires into law have been highly developed, when social communities are extremely fluid, and when leaders are more often made than born, to apply it to the early nineteenth century without reservation is a distinct anachronism.

Yet inevitably the concession theory presupposes that in the early nineteenth century "the support of the masses" had specific electoral effectiveness — at least in certain constituencies. Towards this end it makes a sharp distinction between close constituencies, the corrupt and nomination boroughs, and open constituencies, best exemplified by the English counties.

Granted the social assumptions of the concession theory, the further assumption that these two types of constituency differed from each other basically is an efficient means of explaining the votes of many M.P.'s. The majority of Members for the close constituencies voted against the second Bill on the crucial second reading. Of the eighty-two English county Members only four did so. According to the concession theory this striking disagreement may be attributed, on the one hand, to the entrenched powers of the established ruling classes in the close constituencies, which prevented the free expression of public opinion, and, on the other, to the freedom of the 40s. county freeholders. To balance the bad reputation of the former constituencies historians have endowed the latter with essentially democratic attributes.

Two questions are basic: What determined the electoral behavior of English county voters in 1830 and 1831? And how did the English counties, the open constituencies *par excellence,* differ from the corrupt and nomination boroughs?

To date, these questions — particularly the former — have been accorded but little attention. Yet the poll books, a sadly neglected source for the study of English political and social history, are readily at hand and might suggest answers.

Until 1872, when the Ballot Act separated the voter's name from the vote he cast, voting in England was a public act. After each contested election one or another local political group generally published a list of the local voters, these being identified by their places of residence or their electoral qualification. The electoral choices of each voter were entered in these lists against his name.

The purpose of publishing poll books is clear. So too is their value to historians. By providing a record of electoral behavior poll books allowed the wielders of influence, or their agents, to make sure their influences were not violated. For the historian, who can never know intimately the complexities of influence, poll books measure its effectiveness inadequately. Yet in spite of their inadequacies county poll books do reflect the existence, and to some degree at least, the effectiveness, of influence. They do so in two ways: by showing the degree of electoral agreement on the village level, a level often congruent with the boundaries of an estate, and by showing the intense localism of changes of electoral sentiment. Whenever the overall polls of a county show a change from one election to another, the change is not homogeneous throughout the country. Rather, it is a sum of local changes. Within a locality changes were generally unanimous; from one locality to another such changes were often contradictory.

In circumstances where each voter is free to express his own opinions at the polls — where the modern concept of public opinion is valid — the electoral map of a large geographical constituency will normally consist of shadings from a region where one political group is dominant to another region where another group is dominant. Within these different regions a fair amount of political disagreement will usually exist. No region will be entirely white or entirely black. The differences which define them will consist of shadings of grey.

In the nineteenth century, however, the electoral maps of the English counties were very often spotted, black and white. The Northamptonshire poll book of 1831, for example, shows that all the voters in the village of Lowick polled for the anti-Bill candidates; all the voters in the village of Aldwinkle, directly adjacent to Lowick to the east, polled for the pro-Bill candidates; with two exceptions, all the voters in the village of Brigstock, directly adjacent to Lowick to the northwest, also polled for the pro-Bill candidates. Circumstances suggest that the influences of the dominant local landowners were the major factors both in creating these local communities, and in conditioning the residents' electoral behavior.

Several considerations reinforce this interpretation. Since each elector could cast two votes at each election, he could cast many possible combinations of votes at successive elections. Yet in any particular election local agreement was the general rule. It was so in spite of the utter lack of clearly defined parties, to which, had they existed, such local agreements might possibly be attributed.

But such parties, as distinct from factions, simply did not exist. This is evident both from the large number of plumped votes cast for one candidate who agreed politically with another standing in the same constituency, and also from the large number of split votes between candidates of opposing political views. Even in May 1831 when all of electoral England is supposed to have been divided on the Bill, a large proportion of pro-Bill candidates stood as individuals and were supported as individuals. In Oxfordshire, the two pro-Bill candidates went out of their ways to deny all "coalition." At the polls each enjoyed a few plumped votes and a large number of split votes with the anti-Bill candidate, although understandably, in 1831, such a-political cross-voting was less frequent than usual. . . .

A general picture of non-party, factional politics may be seen in the correspondence of numerous men who had "interests" in one or another county. These men were not unconcerned with "issues." But they were hardly more concerned with "issues" than with gaining the support of Lord This,

Squire That, and Mr. So-and-so for their respective candidates; and often such support had nothing whatsoever to do with "issues." The reasons for their concern are obvious. Sufficient support from such sources might prevent a contest at the polls. In the event that it was not so powerful it would at least do much to determine the electoral result. To attempt to define all the numerous interests of the aristocracy, the squirearchy, and the magnates which affected the outcome of the elections in even one county in 1830 and 1831 would be a sheer impossibility. Evidence could never be found to cover the motives of the crucial score or more men. In the limited number of cases where it is available the evidence tells a story of the hopes and disappointments of those who lived in a world in which ideational elements had not yet displaced the perquisitive. . . .

A distinction must be made between the return of a vast majority of pro-Bill Members to Parliament from the English counties in 1830 and 1831, and the popularity of reform among the English "masses." To a large degree the return of these Members must be attributed to the attitudes and activities of relatively small groups of men, many of them members of the aristocracy, gentry, and urban magnate class, whose composite influences were electorally decisive.

What, then, affected the attitudes of these men?

In 1826 the majority of county Members were Ministerialists because those who wielded the predominant influence in the counties were themselves Ministerialists. Between 1826 and 1831 two things occurred which profoundly affected the political orientation of county Members. In the first place, while many influential Whigs followed obscure convolutions of their own, many influential Tories went into clear opposition. The conjunction of three issues prompted them to do so: the Government's deflationary fiscal policy, the relaxation of the Corn Laws, and Catholic emancipation. In the second place, the urban areas of the counties, which, in general, had previously played a passive political role, awoke from their lethargy.

Growing rural opposition despite many Whigs, and urban awakening, were not opposed; they were allied. The Ultra-Tories, for whom Catholic emancipation was all but equivalent to treason, were especially numerous among the aristocracy and gentry. These groups, composed predominantly of rural landowners, tended to oppose all relaxations of the Corn Laws. They also tended to oppose deflation, regarding it as the main cause of the continuing depression in agriculture. Their doing so placed them in implicit alliance with many manufacturers and provincial bankers, who, like Thomas Attwood, the organizer of the Birmingham Political Union, considered deflation responsible for the urban depression of the latter 'twenties.

Among these issues, Catholic emancipation was the most crucial. The last to arise, and the most heavily charged emotionally, it caught up the hostilities to the Government which the others had already engendered and refocused them upon the entire political structure. Catholic emancipation was the first step towards the first Reform Act not only because, as Professor Briggs notes, it finally dissolved the coalition which Lord Liverpool had held together, but also because it made reform respectable. Numerous Radicals and certain Whigs had long complained of the grossly unrepresentative nature of Parliament. But the questionable associates of many of these men scarcely increased the popularity of reform among the oligarchical wielders of influence. It was the passage of the Catholic Relief Act, and, even more, the manner in which it was passed, which prompted many of these latter first to appraise the political structure of the kingdom and then to add their more effective voices to the cry for reform. Their doing so committed them neither to the democratic theories espoused by some Radicals nor to the liberal views of others who wished to increase the political powers of the urban middle classes. Their

adoption of reform was their way of demanding that the Government remain true to the principles of which they were the major custodians. It was not a legacy of Girondists or Jacobins but of the seventeenth-century Parliamentarians, transmitted through the economical reformers of the reign of George III.

It was to Wellington's apostasy that the passage of the Relief Act was most widely attributed. That Wellington exercised a dominant influence in the Cabinet was agreed by all. That the Cabinet exercised a similar influence in Parliament was suggested to many by the manner in which the Act was passed. Strenuous opposition out of doors was almost entirely discounted in Parliament. In 1829, a significant number of peers and M.P.'s entirely forgot the statements they had made and the votes they had cast the previous year. As the Tory *Morning Herald* bitterly observed, "So much for a measure being recommended by the King and his Ministers, in comparison with a measure emanating from an Opposition side of the House. The King and his Ministers are the fountain-head of power, places, and pensions, and the Opposition is not" (7 Apr. 1829).

From this assumed concentration of power in Wellington's hands the danger arose of what the Tory *Morning Journal* described as Wellington's "proud . . . overbearing . . . grasping . . . dishonest . . . and unprincipled" character (12 Sept. 1829). Their accusation of dishonesty and lack of principle clearly referred to his clandestine change of attitude towards Catholic emancipation between the autumn of 1828 and the meeting of Parliament in 1829. In accusing him of pride and overbearance they alluded to his manner of forcing the Act through Parliament. In accusing him of avarice — and here his supposed lack of principle would also fit — they obviously referred to his refusal to surrender the fruits of the office even though he surrendered the opposition to Catholic emancipation which largely prompted him to accept office in the first place. Looking at emancipation as a whole, many Ultra-Tories asserted that Wellington's continuation in office had become an end in itself which he pursued by every possible means and at the expense, when necessary, of every relevant principle. As an article in *Blackwood's Edinburgh Magazine* explained, "The plea of the Minister — I did this because I could not carry on the government without — is precisely in effect the plea of the pickpocket or murderer — I robbed or murdered because I had no other means of obtaining wealth."

Between the passage of the Relief Act and the elections of 1830, the specific issue of emancipation disappeared almost entirely among the more general issues to which it gave rise; the source of power in Parliament, the nature of that power, the wisdom of its use, and the relations between Parliament and English society. Several things contributed to this process, and contributed, also, to provide the Ultra-Tories with strong allies among the Radicals and rural Whigs. In the first place, in September, Wellington brought suit for libel against the owners of the *Morning Journal,* charging that the paper's comments had tended to bring himself and the Government into contempt. . . . In the second place, the Ministers refused to take seriously the mounting complaints of distress which emanated from countryside and town. Indeed, they asserted through the Speech from the Throne in February 1830 that distress only prevailed "in some parts of the Kingdom." With rebates of agricultural rental increasing throughout the previous autumn, and depression deepening in many towns, such an assertion provoked an even greater outcry than the libel suit. It was on this issue that the Ultra-Tory member for Kent, Sir Edward Knatchbull, moved his amendment to the Address. In the subsequent division the Government was only saved from defeat by the support of certain Liberals and Whigs. . . .

The importance of the Government's attitude towards distress and of the support of certain Liberals and Whigs can hardly be over-emphasized. Many anti-ministerial Tories and many rural Whigs felt confirmed in their views that unless Wellington could be brought to desert his principles once again — but this time in a direction which his past desertions rendered improbable — no efforts would ever be made to deal with distress except after reform. In numerous speeches, articles, and letters to the press from the summer of 1829 through the winter of 1831 the Country Party attacked the theories of the Liberal economists and the increasing adoptions of these theories by the Government. The attack assumed that, given the existing structure of Government, these theories could not be abandoned.

While the Country Party remained an attitude rather than an organization, most of its members were agreed that the ultimate source of England's miseries lay in the conjunction of the national debt, accumulated largely during the French Wars, and the "criminal profusion of Government" (*Morning Herald*, Feb. 4, 1830). While the difficulties of paying war taxes in war currency had been bad enough, Peel had aggravated the problem by a devaluation of the currency, premised on liberal economic theory, which required in practice that debts incurred in paper be repaid in gold. Then, with agriculture and manufacturing nearly prostrate from this burden, Huskisson had made things even worse with his policies of free trade, similarly premised, which forced English producers to compete with foreign producers whose taxes were far lighter.

Some Country Partyites argued that either a simple return to protection or a simple currency reform, or both, would solve their problems. Others, who believed that the dilemma had become far too complex for such a solution to be feasible, pointed to the developing split in the kingdom between those who paid taxes and those who received them in the form of salaries, pensions, or interest. Since those in receipt of taxes in one form or another included the Ministers, their basic supporters in both Houses, and the fundholders, many persons were contemptuous of the Government's professions in favor of retrenchment. The decline of Whig opposition, which many of these men attributed to the eagerness of the Whig leaders to share the spoils of office, led them to proclaim that no relief was possible as long as the structure of government remained unchanged.

Such an interpretation of the kingdom's ills underlay the Tory proposals for reform set forth by the Marquis of Blandford, and by David Robinson in *Blackwood's Edinburgh Magazine*. Neither had a theoretical basis. Each was a practical attempt to deal with a synthesis of practical problems which faced in particular the Country Party. . . .

Where *Blackwood's* stepped cautiously Blandford stamped in anger. His concerns were the same. But he was not satisfied with a simple control of the Ministers' powers. He sought to destroy them. Hence, among his numerous proposals, those to dismiss all placemen and pensioners from the House of Commons and to abolish all nomination boroughs.

While these proposals were being made the Ministers were being pressed in Parliament, primarily by Tories, on such questions as the practice whereby certain Army and Navy officers who took civil posts in the government might continue to receive their full service pay in addition to their civil salaries, pensions for the sons of Cabinet Ministers, distress and the state of the laboring classes, and the salaries of Privy Councillors. But the Country Party had also taken to the field. From the late autumn of 1829 into the following spring they convened a series of county meetings, many of them in the guise of anti-malt tax meetings, at which their leaders ran the gamut of their protest. In January, when the first Political Union was organized, these squires were joined from the towns. The leaders of the Political Unions had similar economic and fiscal concerns from which their reform demands issued. Indeed, of the initial leaders of the Union movement, the majority were anti-ministerial Tories. Blandford joined the parent body almost as soon as it

was organized. His reform proposals were those they later endorsed.

Yet the Union movement was more than an urban amplifier to the growing rural agitation. Its major initial importance was that it provided indigenous political organizations for the urban freeholders.

Traditionally, the counties were controlled from the countryside. In many cases, however, such an arrangement had no basis in electoral reality. In many counties most freeholders were urban. As long as the primary qualification for the county franchise was a 40s. freehold, and as long as most borough freeholders had a county vote, a town such as Birmingham, in which the number of property owners was relatively large, or a borough such as Cambridge was in a position to exercise predominant power in the county in which it was situated. As the *Manchester Mercury* noted on 6 June 1826, while Manchester might have no Member many of its inhabitants had county votes. The later assertion, that two thousand Warwickshire freeholders were concentrated in Birmingham, may have been an exaggeration. Yet it is no exaggeration that in many counties the continued political control of the aristocracy and gentry depended on the continued quiescence of the local urban magnates. It was the burden of the Union movement to underscore the precarious position of the landed interest in the counties.

In 1830, however, in most counties, the precariousness of their position was not yet clear. Yorkshire was exceptional. The Union retained its orientation in favor of the anti-ministerial Tories until well after the elections of August. In these elections, it merely enhanced the powers of the rural anti-Ministerialists. As long as these acted in frequent alliance with the Radicals, and as long as many Whigs and Liberals refrained from attacking Wellington, it was impossible for issues to become polarized in the polemical terms of town *versus* countryside, or middle class *versus* aristocracy.

The results of this activity are to be seen in the elections of August. Tradition notwithstanding, the immediate issues in these elections owed less to the Whigs and Liberals than to the anti-ministerial Tories. The truth of this is nowhere so clearly indicated as when *The Times* described these elections as a contest between the Government and the Ultra-Tory, or Country Party (14 July 1830). However, while the immediate opposition to Wellington came primarily from the Tories, certain of the issues in these elections — retrenchment, freedom of the press, and parliamentary reform — fitted the Foxite Whig, Liberal, and Radical traditions far better than they did the Tory. Hence the tendency to ignore the Tories' role in these elections. Hence, too, the tendency to overlook those other issues which were peculiar to one or more of the various elements of the Country Party — distress, currency reform, and protection. These issues are usually omitted from discussions of reform. Yet the issues to which exclusive attention is usually given had less to do with the developing opposition to Wellington which influenced these elections and which ultimately led to the first Reform Act. . . .

Needing strong speakers in the Commons as well as strong votes, Wellington dallied long with the Canningites. Negotiations with them only broke off when it became apparent they would not join him unless he made room for many Whigs as well. But to have undertaken such a major reorganization of the Cabinet would have meant displacing, and probably offending, a number of faithful men. In view of *The Times'* hostility towards the Whigs before the installation of Grey (e.g., 21 Aug. 1830), and assuming for *The Times* a modicum of the influence it claimed, such a step might have cost Wellington far more than it gained him. In the end he threw his all to the Ultra-Tories. His appeal to them was framed in his denial of the need for political reform.

To regard this denial, as is usually done, as the expression of immovable principle, is to ignore the attitudes of the men with whom Wellington had been negotiating so recently; to some extent, it is to confuse philosophy with tactics. What Wellington clearly sought was the necessary support in Parliament to keep his Government in office. In view of the way in which the Parliamentary parties were later balanced, to have bid for the Ultra-Tories was not unreasonable. This granted, and in view of the movements of one section of opinion in the kingdom, the denial was not capricious — or at least no more so than the change of attitude of *The Times* towards the Whigs between late August and mid-November. With unrest and agitation increasing, and Captain Swing on his nocturnal escapades in Kent, *Blackwood's* had already peered across the channel and seen the specter of universal revolution. So too had the author of the pamphlet, *Tory Union, our only Safeguard against Revolution.* In all probability, Wellington's denial was premised on two assumptions: that the elections marked an Ultra-Tory revival, and that a large enough number of anti-ministerial Tories had been sufficiently scared by the revolution in Paris and the growing economic unrest and radical agitation in England to be willing to support him in carrying on a strong government.

Wellington's denial of the need for reform failed to produce the intended result. That it failed is evidence both of the complexities of reaction to the events in Paris and also of the sincerity of many Tories in their demands for reform. After the *Morning Journal's* attack on Wellington not a few Tories identified themselves less with the fallen minions of Charles X than with his adversaries. When looking to England, these men feared the possibility of a Parisian contagion far less than they did the Government's continued refusal to deal with distress. In November, after the Civil List vote, when many Tories joined in bringing down the Government, the *Morning Herald* explained, "The real question . . . was whether the Representatives of the people of England would, with *pledges of economy* fresh upon their lips, proceed to vote so vast a sum without adopting any

previous inquiry (17 Nov. 1830)." By im-
plication they placed the new session within
the context of the old, for they recognized
neither the Paris revolution nor Wellington's denial as a significant divide. As many
Tories remembered, during the previous
session, Grey, the man most widely touted
as Wellington's probable successor, had declared he had an open mind on the currency question. In announcing the policies
of his Government, Grey promised they
would deal with reform. But he also promised that the relief of distress would be
their "first and most anxious object." With
this combination the *Standard* declared itself satisfied (23 Nov. 1830).

Yet the Paris Revolution and the growing
domestic unrest did mark a break with the
past and Wellington's denial defined it.
The means by which he tried to hold on
to office laid the basis of a new political
polarity which other interests as well as his
own conspired to reinforce. It was one thing
for a coalition of Whigs, Liberals, Canningites, Ultra-Tories, and Radicals to defeat
Wellington; it was another for all but the
Radicals to combine in replacing him. The
several meanings of reform were far too
contradictory for it to provide, as the *Standard* hoped, the basis of a viable coalition
of honest men (23 Nov. 1830). For *The
Times* and the *Standard* to be rivals in adulation of Grey was absurd. Clearly, the
Ministry could not satisfy both. Yet for
these, and other disparate journals, to anticipate satisfaction was not unreasonable.
The *Standard* was quick to recognize the
validity of its arch-opponent's attitude — for
example, Lord Goderich at the Colonial
Office favored free trade. Although it cited
Goderich as well as other men to indicate
that the opinions of which it disapproved
would be held in check — Grey opposed
free trade (23 Nov. 1830) — its doing so
was evidence that its continued support of
Grey was conditional upon his not desert-
ing the *Standard* for its rivals on "the leading journal." That he should do so, however, or that the *Standard* should desert
him, would be to satisfy the forces which

Wellington's denial had loosed upon the
kingdom. Perhaps even more important, in
view of the law that nature prefers spurious
certainty to sincere uncertainty, it would
help define the anomalous coalition in the
Cabinet.

In requiring the Tories who answered his
call to group themselves around the banner
of anti-reform, Wellington effectively
prompted his successors' declaration that
the cause he opposed was the one on which
they would stand or fall. Furthermore, he
prompted the notion that reform should
stand or fall with them. When introducing
the Bill, Lord John Russell was at pains to
explain that the Ministers had taken a position midway between the anti-reformers
and the Radicals. But the party situation
in the winter and spring of 1831 showed
that no such position existed. Former Ministers, sharply divided among themselves,
sought somehow to regroup both their own
party and their would-be allies, while
Whigs, Liberals, and Radicals thundered
for reform in tones whose effect if not
whose motive was to encourage just such a
Tory regroupment. Once the Bill was introduced reform had only one meaning. As
Orator Hunt noted, it was useless to point
out that the Bill "did not contain what the
great mass of petitions . . . had prayed for."
It was equally useless for the *Standard* to
complain of the association between the
political fortunes of Grey and the constitutional future of the kingdom (28. Feb.
1831). Each clause of the Bill was precisely
drafted. Yet for most Englishmen the Bill
was simply the projection of their hopes,
doubts, and fears. Hence the indiscriminate
enthusiasm for the measure in the Whig,
Liberal, and Radical press, and in several
voices of the old Tory press. Hence, too,
the slow regroupment of many of the
Tories. It was such a regroupment, although
far more rapid and complete, which Wellington undoubtedly anticipated in November. In March, when the majority of anti-
ministerial Tories voted against the second
reading of the Bill, regroupment had gone
far enough to allow Wellington to claim

later that had the issue in November been the same as it was in March, he would have remained in office.

While such a claim might allow Wellington to delude himself that it was bad luck which beat him, it entirely neglects the continued chaos among the Tories, the many different reasons which prompted regroupment, and the many other reasons which prompted numerous anti-ministerial Tories either to go into temporary retirement or to remain among their reforming friends. Some Tories who had yearned for Wellington's defeat had second thoughts as the dangers of radical agitation seemed to grow. Others were ill at ease among the "Catholics" of 1829. Others, again, became apprehensive about where the balance had fallen in the Cabinet because nothing was being done to relieve distress. On the basis of Grey's policy statement the *Standard* expected that the relief of distress would precede reform. They began to be concerned when the Ministers announced their intention of introducing a plan of reform without first dealing with distress. Such behavior on the part of the Ministers seemed to imply that under pressure of the liberal economists the relief of distress might be forgotten. If so, they might have dropped from the frying pan into the fire. When Althorp announced that pensions would be continued at the existing rate, when the proposed transfer taxes on funded and landed property were dropped from the budget, largely as a result of fundholder opposition, and when the *Standard* discovered that Poulett Thomson, "the chief representative of the political economists" (18 Feb. 1831), had a hand in drawing up the budget, their dismay was complete. For them, reform was a means of destroying the influence of these men. . . .

The continued coalition of Whigs, Liberals, Radicals, and numerous Tories who supported the Bill was less a measure of the Bill's contents than it was of the implications of Wellington's denial, the consequent identification of reform with the Grey Ministry, and, for many Tories, the

continued validity of their arguments of the previous year. In those few counties where the elections were contested the reformers' singleness of purpose was enhanced by the influence they wielded in the towns. Elsewhere, this influence undoubtedly went a long way to explain their opponents' reluctance to contest.

Referring to these county elections, Alison's article probably exaggerated the degree of rural opposition to the Bill. . . . But in any case, as both the summer and Tory regroupment progressed, and as the tactical effects wore off of identifying reform with the Grey Ministry, the electoral fortunes of the Bill's opponents changed sharply. Between the end of May and the end of October, anti-Bill candidates — either anti-reformers or moderates — won every contested by-election but one, that in Cambridgeshire. They gained a total of ten new seats.

When Grey's colleagues observed these elections and the growth of anti-Bill sentiment in the City they were deeply disturbed. Having asserted their claim to office in terms of the electoral mandate of May, they feared lest such "proof of reaction [against reform, or of] preference for a measure more moderate than [their own]" should prompt the king to dismiss them. In these circumstances they discussed the possibility of appealing for a new mandate, born of violence, that would derive from the "fears" of the king and their opponents. It may be impossible either to prove or disprove the possible complicity of certain Ministers in the riots which occurred in the autumn of 1831. But it was then that the riots to which the concession theorists have subsequently pointed began in earnest.

Clearly, these riots had much to do with the king's decision not to dismiss Grey after the Lords turned down the Bill in October. Subsequent demonstrations undoubtedly prompted him to reinstate Grey after he had dismissed him the following spring, and to promise him the necessary peers to pass the Bill. But the Bill had already been drafted. Thus, the relevance of these riots and demonstrations to the Bill itself is far less clear than their relevance to the political consequences of Wellington's denial.

It is true that the riots were directed against the Tory leaders in Parliament, and that these men were the main organizers of opposition to the Bill. Yet these men were scarcely agreed in their attitudes towards reform. Some were concerned primarily with the political or constitutional implications of the Bill, the loss of ministerial power which would result from such abolition of the grosser nomination boroughs as the Ministers proposed. To many others, however, these implications were not unattractive. What most disturbed them were the social implications of the measure, how it would affect the future relations between the landed and the urban interests.

Wellington's denial, the consequent political polarity, and the numerous Radical demonstrations, provided the context for a polemical redefinition of reform in social terms which helped drive many Country Partyites back into his arms. As such, his denial was belatedly successful: it obscured the distinction between the two Tory groups. In doing so, it lent credence to his assertion that the issue at stake was not the power of the Government but the survival of the landed interest.

Yet if the real issue of the Bill had been the social one, the future of the landed interest would have been sad indeed. In the late spring of 1831 the political weakness of the opponents of the Bill was patent. The vast majority of members for the counties and open boroughs were its ardent supporters. Almost alone the members for the close boroughs opposed it and many of these boroughs were scheduled for abolition. If the Bill itself reflected the pressures for reform to which the concession theorists have generally attributed its passage — the demands of the urban middle classes for a voice in political affairs, and the threats of mob violence if their demands went unanswered — then 1832 should have inaugurated a major social revolution in the House of Commons. But nothing of the sort occurred. Indeed, while the polemical arguments which conceived of reform in social terms were shouted from many hustings, the majority of members had been drawn before. In voting for the Bill these men did not commit social treason. As Russell had tried vainly to explain, the Bill was alien to the background of radical agitation. As Palmerston pointedly observed, possibly having in mind the growth of urban organization in the counties which derived largely from the Political Unions, the Bill "went to *restore* to the landed interest that influence which he thought indispensable . . . to the safety and prosperity of the country."

A detailed analysis of the ways in which the first Reform Act effectively restored the political powers of the landed interest is beyond the scope of this paper. However, these points may be noted: the Act withdrew certain constituencies from the control of the Government; it withdrew others from the control, or significant influence, of urban leaders.

By disfranchising or reducing the representation of the smallest boroughs, those from which Wellington's power had largely derived, the Grey Ministry gained a redistribution fund of over one hundred and forty seats. Of these, they assigned sixty-four seats to new English boroughs, primarily in the industrial north. However, the social significance of the Act tends to be distorted unless these new borough seats are balanced against the political redefinition of the English counties and the assignment to them of sixty-two new seats.

Two important aspects of the elections of 1830 and 1831 were the growth and decline of reform sentiment among the aristocracy and gentry, and the emergence of urban leaders in the arena of county politics. In 1831 urban leaders played prominent parts in returning the majority of the eighty-two English county members. The basis of their doing so lay in the relative electoral weights of the urban areas of the counties. In large measure the Act destroyed these relative weights. Thus, while urban leaders retained control of the majority of the sixty-odd seats for open boroughs which existed before 1832, and gained control of the majority of the sixty-four new borough seats, rural leaders were restored to predominant control in the majority of the eighty-two pre-reform English county seats and provided with an additional sixty-two new county seats. Unless Wellington's assertion be allowed — which, after the legislation of the previous years, many peers and more squires would hardly have done — that the nomination boroughs were the true defenders of the landed interest, on balance the landed interest came out ahead.

The Grey Ministry made no secret of their intentions regarding the English counties. In introducing the first Bill, Russell declared that the counties should be isolated from the towns so that these might not "interfere with the representation of the counties." In part this isolation was achieved by means of new electoral qualifications, in part by enfranchising new boroughs.

Before 1832, urban interference in the counties was primarily the result of most urban freeholders' being qualified as county electors. As has been seen, before 1832 many counties were electorally urban. After 1832, in most counties, the rural balance was significantly increased. This was achieved in large measure by two complementary procedures. First, the urban elements in the county electorates were reduced by enacting new borough qualifications, by providing that a freehold property in a borough should not convey a county franchise if it conveyed a borough franchise, and by granting new borough status to many of the larger towns. Second, the rural elements in the county electorates were increased by enfranchising certain copyholders and leaseholders, and by accepting the Chandos clause, which extended the right to vote to tenants at will.

The rural and aristocratic nature of the counties was still further enhanced by the means adopted of increasing their overall representation in Parliament. The Ministers suggested that most of the counties be cut into two divisions, each to return two members, and that a third member be given to all but a few of the others. As far as the Ministers were concerned, such divisions, besides increasing the number of county Members, would also increase the localism of county politics. It was Althorp's boast that this localism would weaken the tendency of certain counties to return persons on the basis of their "mere popularity."

The provisions of the measure which sought to reduce the expense of county elections involved a number of technical points of electioneering practice which are too complicated to examine in the present paper. However, they too were conceived as a means of increasing the effective powers of local oligarchs.

The similarity of intent is clear between these various provisions of the Act and the earlier suggestions of the Marquis of Blandford and articles in *Blackwood's Edinburgh Magazine*. This is not to suggest that the committee which drew up the ministerial plan took their cue from the Tories. It is to suggest that the polemical arguments which conceived of reform in social terms were largely irrelevant.

This paper does not tell the whole story of the Bill. Even less does it tell the whole story of reform. It does, however, suggest aspects of these phenomena which historians have tended to ignore: that they are far too complex to be satisfactorily described within a simplified revolutionary framework. Not only did the Bill provide an enlarged number of constituencies for representatives of the urban middle classes, it also clarified the political powers of the landed classes, the aristocracy and gentry. As their own regroupment progressed these classes settled back to a half century during which their control was absolute in the majority of the remaining small boroughs, and in all English county divisions except those in which significant urban populations lacked borough representation of their own. In practical terms, the first Reform Act was far less a blow against the powers in the State of the aristocracy and gentry than it was against the powers of the Ministers.

This realization caused dismay to some Whigs, and to many Liberals and Radicals when, as early as 1835, certain traits of the child they had claimed as their own became apparent. Their dismay is not to be wondered at. They were the disillusioned victims of one of the first of the numerous propaganda wars of the nineteenth century.

Yet while these men had not gained what they sought, they had not entirely lost. To enhance the independence of members of Parliament from Ministerial control was not to transfer power away from the ruling oligarchies. Rather, it was to transfer power from Whitehall to the constituencies. There it resided during the middle years of the century until the development of centralized political parties brought it back. But the transfer of power effected by the Act provided that whenever local control changed hands, or local leaders changed their attitudes, such changes would be reflected in Parliament.

In view of the use to which Ministerial power had been put in the years before 1832 — to emancipate Catholics, to liberalize the Corn Laws, and in view, also, of the Radicals' subsequent impatience with Parliament the question arises of the relationship between the Reform Act and later "bourgeois" legislation. As observers after 1832 were not slow to notice, legislation became increasingly responsive to changes of "public opinion." Such changes, however, are far slower, far more cumbersome, than those initiated by the spark of an idea within a fairly intimate group of fairly intelligent men.

The fondness of the Benthamites for Wellington and Peel in 1829 and 1830 may, indeed, be extremely significant. If history followed a logical progression (which it never does), it might be argued that the first Reform Act did more to delay such measures as the repeal of the Corn Laws than it did to accelerate them.

SUGGESTIONS FOR ADDITIONAL READING

The standard work for the Reform Bill of 1832 is J. R. M. Butler's *The Passing of the Great Reform Bill* (London, 1914). His account emphasizes the economic, social, and political pressures for political reform, and the interpretation presented is a social-psychological one of the reform movement of 1830–1832. For the student who cannot get to English newspaper source materials, Mr. Butler quotes liberally from *The Times, Morning Chronicle, Standard, Morning Herald, Morning Post* and *Globe*. The ideological bias of these newspapers can be identified in A. A. Aspinall's *Politics and the Press, 1780–1850* (London, 1948).

The development of the controversy over reform can be followed in the pages of such periodicals as the *Edinburgh Review*, the *Quarterly Review*, the *Westminster Review*, and *Blackwood's Edinburgh Magazine*. The *Edinburgh Review* speaks for the Whigs and the *Westminster Review* for the Benthamite Radicals; the *Quarterly Review* defends the Tory position and *Blackwood's* represents the ultra-Tories. The positions on reform taken by the political leaders of the day and spokesmen for particular interests can be found in *Hansard's Parliamentary Debates*, 3rd Series. Asa Briggs and Norman Gash have contributed articles on the local history of the Reform Bill struggle. Such studies are Norman Gash, "Brougham and the Yorkshire Election of 1830," *Proceedings of the Leeds Philosophical Society*, VIII (1956). Asa Briggs, "The Background of the Parliamentary Reform Movement in Three English Cities," *Cambridge Historical Journal*, X (1952), 293–317, is a classic, as are his "Thomas Atwood and the Economic Background of the Birmingham Political Union," *Cambridge Historical Journal*, IX (1948), 190–216; and "Social Structure and politics in Birmingham and Lyons, 1825–48," *British Journal of Sociology*, I (1950), 67–80.

Annotated bibliographies of the period can be found in E. L. Woodward, *Age of Reform, 1815–1870* (London, 1962); and A. A. Aspinall and E. Anthony Smith (eds.), *English Historical Documents, Vol. II, 1783–1832* (London, 1959). Norman Gash, *Politics in the Age of Peel* (London, 1953) has interesting chapters on the English, Scottish, and Irish reform acts.

There are excellent chapters on reform in the following general histories: Spencer Walpole, *History of England from the Conclusion of the Great War in 1815*, 6 vols. (London, 1890); Élie Halévy, *History of the English People in the Nineteenth Century*, 6 vols. (London, 1949–1952); J. A. R. Marriott, *England since Waterloo* (London, 1913; G. M. Trevelyan, *England in the Nineteenth Century and After* (London, 1937); E. L. Woodward, *Age of Reform* (London, 1962); and Asa Briggs, *The Age of Improvement* (London, 1959). John A. Roebuck, *History of the Whig Ministry of 1830* (London, 1852) and William Nassau Molesworth, *History of England from the Year 1830–1874*, 3 vols. (London, 1871–1873) are accounts of reform by Radical supporters of the Reform Act. Molesworth has tables of the constituencies — their electorate and influence — that were to lose one or two seats in Lord John Russell's Bill of 1831. Joseph Hamburger, *James Mill and the Art of Revolution* (New Haven, 1963), has an interesting chapter on the role of the press and voluntary associations in the agitation for parliamentary reform, as does Henry Ferguson, "The Birmingham Politicals and the Government, 1831–1832," *Victorian Studies*, III (1960), 261–276. The two best recent articles on the Reform Act are D. C. Moore, "The Other Face of Reform," *Victorian Studies*, V (1961–1962), 7–34, and "Concession or Cure: The Sociological Premises of the First Reform Act," *The Historical Journal*, IX (1966), 39–59.

Details on the workings of the pre-reform

Parliament can be found in William Gwyn, *Democracy and the Cost of Politics in Britain* (London, 1962), and Edward and A. G. Porritt, *The Unreformed House of Commons,* 2 vols. (Cambridge, 1909). Butler's *The Passing of the Great Reform Bill,* cited above, also has much information on this topic. Betty Kemp treats the relationship between the House of Commons and the Crown in *King and Commons, 1660–1832* (London, 1957). A. S. Foord discusses "The Waning of the Influence of the Crown," *English Historical Review,* LXII (1948), 484–507, and A. S. Turberville the power of the Lords in *The House of Lords in the Age of Reform, 1784–1837* (London, 1958). Sir Lewis Namier, *The Structure of Politics at the Accession of George III* (London, 1957), is a solid methodological study of the structure of politics in the eighteenth century. G. S. Veitch, *The Genesis of Parliamentary Reform* (London, 1913), and Anthony Brown, *The French Revolution in English History* (London, 1918) trace the origins of the parliamentary reform movement back to the mid-eighteenth century.

Many of the leaders of the Reform Bill struggle and their close friends have left memoirs which furnish insight into the period. Lord Grey's son, Henry, edited his father's correspondence with the King in *The Reform Act: the Correspondence of the late Earl Grey with His Majesty King William IV . . . from November 1830 to June 1832,* 2 vols. (London, 1867); and Rollo Russell compiled the papers of his father, one of the members of the Committee of Four, in *The Early Correspondence of Lord Russell, 1805–1840,* 2 vols. (London, 1913). Lord John Russell, himself, offered *Recollections and Suggestions, 1813–1873* (London, 1875). Lord Brougham supplied his own account of the period in the *Life and Times of Henry, Lord Brougham,* 3 vols. (New York, 1871). Other memoirs are: A. R. Wellesley, Duke of Wellington, *Despatches, Correspondence and Memoranda of the Duke of Wellington,* 3d Series, 1819–1832, 8 vols. (London, 1867–1880); C. S. Parker, *Sir Robert Peel from his Private Correspondence and Papers,* 3 vols. (London, 1881–1899); and C. S. Parker, *Life and Letters of Sir James Graham,* 2 vols. (London, 1907); Lord Broughton, *Recollections of a Long Life,* 4 vols. (London, 1910); Stuart Reid, *Life and Letters of Lord Durham,* 2 vols. (London, 1906); *Journal of Mrs. Arbuthnot, 1820–1832,* 2 vols. edited by Francis Bamford and the Duke of Wellington (London, 1950); A. A. Aspinall, *Three Early Nineteenth Century Diaries* (London, 1952); *The Creevey Papers,* edited by Sir Herbert Maxwell, 2 vols. (London, 1904); *The Croker Papers,* edited by L. J. Jennings, 3 vols. (London, 1884); and *The Greville Memoirs,* edited by Lytton Strachey and Roger Fulford, 8 vols. (London, 1938).

Among the studies of leading political figures in the Reform Bill struggle are G. M. Trevelyan's outstanding *Lord Grey and the Reform Bill* (London, 1920); Chester W. New, *Lord Durham* (Oxford, 1929); Leonard Cooper, *Radical Jack* (London, 1959); G. T. Garratt, *Lord Brougham* (London, 1935); A. A. Aspinall, *Lord Brougham and the Whig Party* (London, 1927); Frances Hawes, *Henry Brougham* (New York, 1958); Chester W. New, *Life of Henry Brougham to 1830* (Oxford, 1961); Bertram Newman, *Lord Melbourne* (London, 1930); David Cecil, *Melbourne* (New York, 1939); Philip Guedalla, *Wellington* (London, 1931); Norman Gash, *Mr. Secretary Peel* (Cambridge, 1961); A. A. W. Ramsay, *Sir Robert Peel* (London, 1928); Arvel B. Erickson, *The Public Career of Sir James Graham* (Cleveland, 1952); Myron F. Brightfield, *John Wilson Crocker* (Berkeley, California, 1940); Spencer Walpole, *Life of Lord John Russell* (London, 1889); A. Wyatt Tilby, *Lord John Russell* (London, 1930); Melville W. Patterson, *Sir Francis Burdett and His Times, 1770–1844,* 2 vols. (London, 1931); *The Life and Struggles of William Lovett, An Autobiography* (London, 1876); Jessie K. Buckley, *Joseph Parkes of Birmingham* (London, 1926); Mrs. Millicent Fawcett, *Life of the Right Hon. Sir William Molesworth* (London, 1901); Graham Wallas, *Life of Francis Place* (London, 1918); Samuel Bamford, *Passages in the Life of a Radical*, 2 vols. (London, 1844); and Edward Baines, *The Life and Times of Edward Baines* (London, 1851).

Important developments in party organiation and the party system can be followed in: A. A. Aspinall, "English Party Organization in the Early 19th Century," *English Historical Review*, XLI (1926), 389–411; K. G. Feiling, *The Second Tory Party, 1714–1832* (London, 1951); H. W. C. Davis, *The Age of Grey and Peel* (Oxford, 1929); G. Kitson Clark, *Peel and the Conservative Party* (London, 1929); R. B. McCallum, *The Liberal Party from Earl Grey to Asquith* (London, 1963); and Donald Southgate, *The Passing of the Whigs, 1832–1886* (London, 1962). Three very important works of Norman Gash should also be noted: Norman Gash, *Politics in the Age of Peel*, already cited; "Peel and the Party System, 1830–1850," *Transactions, Royal Historical Society, 5th Series*, I (1951), 47–69; and his Ford lectures of 1964, *Reaction and Reconstruction in English Politics, 1832–1852* (Oxford, 1965). For a discussion of parties and issues in the 1840's, see W. O. Aydelotte, "Party and Issues in Early Victorian England," *Journal of British Studies*, V (1966), 95–114.

Several studies of the post-Reform Bill House of Commons have been done: S. F. Woolley reviews "The Personnel of the Parliament of 1833," *English Historical Review*, LIII (1938), 240–262. W. O. Aydelotte studies the social composition of the Parliament of 1841–1847 in three substantial articles: "The House of Commons in the 1840's," *History*, XXXIX (1954), 249–262; "A Statistical Analysis of the Parliament of 1841: Some Problems of Method," *Bulletin of the Institute of Historical Research*, XXVII (1954), 142–144; "Voting Patterns in the British House of Commons in the 1840's," *Comparative Studies in Society and History*, V (1963), 134–163. J. A. Thomas attempts the same kind of study, with a less sophisticated methodology, in *The House of Commons, 1831–1901* (Cardiff, 1937).

Professor Aydelotte's article, "The Country Gentlemen and the Repeal of the Corn Laws," *English Historical Review*, LXXXIII (1967), 47–60, reviews the important historiographical works on Corn Law repeal. These include three works by G. Kitson Clark, "The Electorate and the Repeal of the Corn Laws," *Transactions, Royal Historical Society, 5th Series*, I (London, 1951), 109–126; "The Repeal of the Corn Laws and the Politics of the Forties," *Economic History Review*, 2d Series, IV (1951), 1–13; *The Making of Victorian England* (London, 1962). Other studies are Norman McCord, *The Anti-Corn Law League 1838–46* (London, 1958); Betty Kemp, "Reflections on the Repeal of the Corn Laws," *Victorian Studies*, V (1962), 189–204; George L. Mosse, "The Anti-League, 1844–46," *Economic History Review*, XVII (1947), 134–142; Mary Lawson-Tancred, "The Anti-League and the Corn Law Crisis of 1846," *Historical Journal*, III (1960), 162–183; and David Spring, "Earl Fitzwilliam and the Corn Laws," *American Historical Review*, LIX (1954), 287–304.

The Irish question led to political reform in 1832 and to economic reform in 1846. On the other hand, immediately after 1832 and again in 1848, the Irish question stalled reform. Asa Briggs in his *Age of Improvement*, cited above, discusses the relationship of "Cash, Corn and Catholics," the famous three C's of the 1820's. Other important studies of the Irish question are: G. I. T. Machin, *The Catholic Question in English Politics, 1820–1830* (Oxford, 1964) and by the same author, "The Maynooth Grant, the Dissenters and Disestablishment, 1845–47," *English Historical Review*, LXXXII (1967), 61–85; Lawrence McCaffrey, *Daniel O'Connell and the Repeal Year* (Kentucky, 1966); Cecil Woodham Smith, *The Great Hunger* (London, 1962); Kevin

B. Nowlan, *The Politics of Repeal* (Toronto, 1965); David Large, "The House of Lords and Ireland in the Age of Peel, 1832–1850," *Irish Historical Studies*, IX (1955), 368–399; *The Great Famine*, ed. by R. Dudley Edwards and T. Desmond Williams (New York, 1957); and two articles by Gilbert A. Cahill, "Irish Catholicism and English Toryism," *Review of Politics*, XIX (1957), 62–76; and "The Protestant Association and the Anti-Maynooth Agitation of 1845," *Catholic Historical Review*, XLIII (1957), 273–308. Two works which relate the Irish question to the demise of chartism are: A. R. Schoyen, *The Chartist Challenge* (London, 1958); and F. C. Mather, *Chartism* (London, Historical Association, 1965).

G. Lowes Dickinson in the *Development of Parliament in the Nineteenth Century* (London, 1895) contends that the Act of 1867 was the culmination of a development that had been continuous since the agitation for the first Reform Bill. The best historiographical essay on the Act of 1867 is by Gertrude Himmelfarb, "The Politics of Democracy: the English Reform Act of 1867," *Journal of British Studies*, VI (1966), 97–138. She cites two articles by Francis H. Herrick, "The Reform Bill of 1867 and the British Party System," *Pacific Historical Review*, III (1934), 216–233; and "The Second Reform Movement in Britain," *Journal of the History of Ideas*, IX (1948), 174–192. Also noted are: Frances E. Gillespie, *Labor and Politics in England, 1850–67* (Durham, N. C., 1927); Joseph H. Park, *The English Reform Bill of 1867* (New York, 1920); Charles Seymour, *Electoral Reform in England and Wales* (New Haven, 1915); Asa Briggs, *Victorian People* (London, 1954); Trygve R. Tholfsen, "The Transition to Democracy in Victorian England," *International Review of Social History*, VI (1961), 226–248; Samuel Beer, *British Politics in the Collectivist Age* (New York, 1966). The most recent book on the Act of 1867 is F. B. Smith, *The Making of the Second Reform Bill* (Cambridge, 1967). Robert Blake's *Disraeli* (London, 1967) is also worth reading.